THE JOURNAL OF
CORPORATE
CITIZENSHIP

Issue 60
December 2015

Theme Issue: **Pretoria Leadership Conference**

Guest Editor:

Derick de Jongh, University of Pretoria, South Africa

ISBN: 978-1-78353-359-6

---

print ISSN 1470-5001   *online* ISSN 2051-4700

Greenleaf
PUBLISHING

THE JOURNAL OF CORPORATE CITIZENSHIP

General Editor Professor Malcolm McIntosh

Regional Editor North America: Professor Sandra Waddock, Boston College, Carroll School of Management, USA

Publisher Anna Comerford, Greenleaf Publishing, UK
Production Editor Sadie Gornall-Jones, Greenleaf Publishing, UK

CORRESPONDENCE

The Journal of Corporate Citizenship encourages response from its readers to any of the issues raised in the journal. All correspondence is welcomed and should be sent to the General Editor c/o Greenleaf Publishing, Aizlewood's Mill, Nursery St, Sheffield S3 8GG, UK; jcc@greenleaf-publishing.com.

All content should be submitted via **online submission**. For more information see the journal homepage at www.greenleaf-publishing.com/jcc.

Books to be considered for review should be marked for the attention of the Book Review Editor c/o Greenleaf Publishing, Aizlewood's Mill, Nursery St, Sheffield S3 8GG, UK; jcc@greenleaf-publishing.com.

- All articles published in *The Journal of Corporate Citizenship* are assessed by an external panel of business professionals, consultants and academics.

- *The Journal of Corporate Citizenship* is indexed with and included in: **Cabells, EBSCO, ProQuest,** the **Association of Business Schools Academic Journal Guide, ABDC** and **Journalseek.net.** It is monitored by 'Political Science and Government Abstracts' and 'Sociological Abstracts'.

SUBSCRIPTION RATES

The Journal of Corporate Citizenship is a quarterly journal, appearing in March, June, September and December of each year. Cheques should be made payable to Greenleaf Publishing and sent to the address below.

Annual online subscription
Individuals: £80.00/€112.50/US$150.00
Organizations: £540.00/€650.00/US$850.00

Annual print and online subscription
Individuals: £90.00/€120.00/US$160.00
Organizations: £550.00/€672.50/US$860.00

Annual print subscription
Individuals: £80.00/€112.50/US$150.00
Organizations: £180.00/€240.00/US$320.00

The Journal of Corporate Citizenship
Greenleaf Publishing Ltd, Aizlewood Business Centre, Aizlewood's Mill, Nursery Street, Sheffield S3 8GG, UK
Tel: +44 (0)114 282 3475   Fax: +44 (0)114 282 3476   Email: jcc@greenleaf-publishing.com.
Or order from our website: www.greenleaf-publishing.com/jcc.

ADVERTISING

The Journal of Corporate Citizenship will accept a strictly limited amount of display advertising in future issues. It is also possible to book inserts. Suitable material for promotion includes publications, conferences and consulting services. For details on rates and availability, please email jcc@greenleaf-publishing.com.

FSC
www.fsc.org
MIX
Paper from
responsible sources
FSC® C013604

Printed in the UK on environmentally friendly, acid-free paper from managed forests by CPI Group (UK) Ltd, Croydon

DOI: [10.9774/GLEAF.4700.2015.de.00002]

Editorial

Issue 60 *December 2015*

Malcolm McIntosh

General Editor, Journal of Corporate Citizenship

AIRPORT BOOKSHOPS AND AMAZON HAVE a proliferation of books on leadership, divided between those following someone who has led and succeeded in their particular field, with their particular way, and any number of things you can do every day to make you a leader. Looking at individuals, we could cite Mahatma Gandhi and Nelson Mandela, Bill Gates and Steve Jobs, Adolf Hitler and Winston Churchill. But much more interesting is studying the tides of history and the evidence of collectivization for the common good in human affairs: for we are social beings, and it is through working together that we achieve most. Since 1945 we have learnt to talk before fighting, to negotiate rather than going to war, and we have recognized the necessity of teaching the skills of social capital development rather than aggressive intervention. But, looking around the world we see many places where men, and it is mostly men, posture with their antlers up high. And we see that transparency is still one of the first principles of corporate responsibility (VW and the Catholic Church are but the latest instances of corporate lying and denial).

This collection of *JCC* papers from a conference in Pretoria led by Derick de Jongh are a contribution to thinking in the large area of leadership. Brutus says in Shakespeare's *Julius Caesar*: "There is a tide in the affairs of men. / Which, taken at the flood, leads on to fortune; / Omitted, all the voyage of their life / Is bound in shallows and in miseries. / On such a full sea are we now afloat, / And we must take the current when it serves, / Or lose our ventures." We have reached a moment in the affairs of (men) when we must collectively seize the moment, for while we talk of business and management, equality and egalitarianism, trade and partnerships, now is the moment to reverse the course of the current model of industrial capitalism and reach a kinder accommodation with ourselves and the Earth.

Founding Editor, of the
Journal of Corporate Citizenship

Author of *Thinking the Twenty-First Century: Ideas for the New Political Economy* (2015)

Malcolm McIntosh
Bath, England
July 2015

DOI: [10.9774/GLEAF.4700.2015.de.00003]

Guest Editorial

The 3rd International Conference on Responsible Leadership*

Issue 60 *December 2015*

Derick de Jongh
University of Pretoria, South Africa

IN THIS GUEST EDITORIAL I WILL FIRST AIM TO provide the context for the decision on the theme for the 3rd International Conference that was hosted in November 2014 in Pretoria, South Africa. Second, I will argue why responsible leadership as an emerging discourse should be considered from an inter-disciplinary (if not trans-disciplinary) point of view, and then I will provide an overview of articles appearing in this issue. Finally, this editorial argues for more active deliberation among academics on moving the level of analysis of leadership theory beyond the individual level to the collective level, bearing in mind multiple role-players and academic disciplines.

The Albert Luthuli Centre for Responsible Leadership (ALCRL) and the Globally Responsible Leadership Initiative, along with international conference partners Griffith University Business School, Business School Lausanne, Tongji SEM, and Babson College, invited papers related to responsible leadership from a trans-disciplinary perspective involving the social and natural sciences. These papers were reviewed against its alignment with the conference theme "Bridging science, business and politics: the role of responsible leadership in creating the necessary transition to a sustainable global economy". Fifty-one abstracts were received and reviewed.

* I would like to express my sincere appreciation to Professor Malcolm McIntosh, the General Editor of the *Journal of Corporate Citizenship*, for not only supporting this special issue but also being instrumental in deciding on the conference theme and drafting the announcement for the 3rd International Conference. Many of his specific conceptual ideas appear in this guest editorial. I would also like to thank Professor Sandra Waddock, who was instrumental in scoping the conference theme and contributing to the call for papers; many of her ideas also appear in this guest editorial. The team at Greenleaf Publishing also need a special mention for managing the overall process with such professionalism—Anna Comerford and Rhian Williams. Lastly, I would like to acknowledge Siyapiwa Maphanga's assistance in writing this editorial.

Twenty abstracts made the first cut and their authors were requested to submit full papers. Through a double-blind review process, 15 papers made it through this round and their authors were invited to present them at the conference. These 15 papers were published in the conference proceedings and, from these, five papers were finally selected, after a second round of double-blind review, to appear in this special edition.

Reality check

I would like to argue that a current, relevant and appropriate starting point for an editorial making the case for bridging science, business and politics and highlighting the role of responsible leadership is the recent unfolding of the Volkswagen (VW) scandal. An article in the *Economist* (September 2015) expresses opinions on the magnitude of this scandal, predicting systemic shock that might lead to reshaping the industry as a whole. Reshaping the industry does not sound like a bad idea, on condition that it is done in a responsible manner.

Although one can argue that it might have been the very scientists at VW who manipulated technology in support of sales targets, it could have been an MBA graduate in a managerial position with little if any ethical inclination. Be that as it may, it places the role of science in our striving for a sustainable world under the proverbial spotlight. But then again, the general assumption that science is a value-free discipline is untrue in this context. Science is compromised through its agendas, which are mostly driven by the client's/employer's expectations, rather than the individual scientist's personal principles. A report by the WWF-UK (Crompton, 2010) argues that the "enlightened model" of human decision-making is extremely incomplete. This would apply particularly in the context of scientific objectives and decisions, much as one would like to believe that science should be sovereign and independent. Unfortunately, the recent VW case offers proof that the decisions made by the VW engineers were extremely biased, in that they were based on the interests of only one group of stakeholders, the shareholders and owners of VW. Unfortunately, in the complex world we live in, "enlightened" decision-making would only be found in the ideal case where the common good supersedes self-interest.

Scientific innovation is indeed crucial in the context of these large-scale and complex problems. Voegtlin and Scherer (2014) point out that scientific innovation should do no harm to people and the planet but should be done in the interest of the common good. They also argue that global governance schemes should be in place to facilitate scientific progress. The case of VW bears testimony to the complete opposite. The intention of that scientific innovation was, on the contrary, to do harm and bypass governance systems. In all this, the obvious and critical question to be answered is: what was the position of the VW leaders in all of this?

Freeman and Auster (2011) note that scholars are calling for responsible leadership to become the norm, and point out that organizations are being pushed to demonstrate values of responsibility and sustainability by paying more attention to the implications of their actions on society as a whole. The spotlight should therefore fall on the role of scientists in these organizations in solving complex social and environmental problems and, more importantly, the role of (responsible) leadership. Only time will tell to what extent VW will be able to redeem itself and show real, responsible leadership in years to come.

Background and introduction

Responsible leadership should, in my view, be seen as an emerging discourse. As much as some might argue that it is becoming a major theme in management sciences (Stahl and De Luque, 2014), my reading of the literature and review of opinion pieces by academics and non-academics has convinced me that it is still a field in its infancy. I would therefore like to argue that it should rather be viewed as a "communal holding space" in which critical management and leadership scientists and practitioners can debate the issue of responsibility in the context of what it implies for leadership as a whole. Maak and Pless (2006) support this by presenting responsible leadership as a social-relational and ethical phenomenon, which occurs in social processes of interaction. In a position paper by Mervis et al. (2010), arguing for responsible leadership as an emerging discourse, responsible (business) leadership is viewed as a phenomenon that shapes, and is being shaped by, a complex adaptive process involving individuals, organizations and societies. Many leaders and organizations are transforming

from a traditional hierarchical model of responsibility to a contemporary, more relational approach. It is this relational dimension within which I position responsible leadership that warrants the emphasis being placed on inter-disciplinarity.

To further support this viewpoint, if one considers the levels of analysis in leadership research, Dionne et al. (2014) found that owing to the increase in the complexity of organizational sciences and their implications for multi-level relations, leadership research should be carried out within multi-level frameworks. One could also describe these multi-level frameworks as multi-disciplinary, multi-sector, moving from the individual, to the dyadic, to the collective level. This argument correlates with Mervis et al.'s view that responsible leadership is a complex adaptive process involving multiple levels. With reference to the rationale for deciding on the theme of this conference, responsible leadership can therefore be viewed as a cross-cutting phenomenon, suggesting some kind of bridging role between science, business and politics. The conference was therefore situated in a trans-disciplinary context.

As the interconnectedness and complexity of the world continues to grow, there is increasing awareness of the limitations of knowledge gathered within strict disciplinary boundaries, just at the point when humanity is pushing beyond many planetary boundaries and limitations. The result is an enhanced need for responsible leaders whose knowledge and wisdom transcends disciplinary, sector and most current boundaries. Voegtlin (2015), however, argues that "responsibility" is the missing element in our understanding, expectations and experiences of leaders. He draws on the work of Young (2011), who considers responsibility within the liability model, assigning responsibility to particular agents whose actions can be causally connected to the circumstances for which responsibility is sought. If we replace "agents" in this context with people in leadership positions (scientific, business and political), it becomes even clearer that responsibility stretches far beyond immediate and individual circumstances to long-term and societal interests and circumstances.

Management, leadership and business knowledge by itself cannot ensure a sustainable and equitable future. Scientific knowledge alone is not enough, especially when it can be compromised, as in the VW case. Knowledge of governance and political science alone is also not enough. What is needed is an integration of knowledge about and insight into responsible leadership across disciplinary boundaries, ranging from management and economics studies, the physical and biological sciences, to law, government, and the humanities and social science. Only by integrating across current disciplinary boundaries can we find hope for generating what has been termed "earth system governance", a way for humanity to manage the complexities of the world to create a just, equitable and sustainable world for all.

Bierman (2007, p. 326) argues, however, that earth system management is vaguely defined since it is "too elusive for natural scientists and too ambitious and normative for social scientists". He argues that earth systems governance is a new social phenomenon, a political programme and a cross-cutting theme of research in the field of global environmental change, grounded in social science theory. This view supports the need to consider responsible leadership as a socially constructed phenomenon (Maak and Pless, 2006) and, more specifically, to consider how this understanding of responsible leadership fits into the earth system governance principle.

The manifold ecological, biodiversity, equity and sustainability problems of the world necessitate new and integrated scientific understanding in a whole range of biological and physical science disciplines. But siloed scientific knowledge alone will be insufficient to effect necessary changes in the systems and cultures of humankind's economic and political systems. Shrivastava et al. (2013, p. 230) argue in support of transdisciplinarity, which "offers unique real-world problem solving that crosses disciplinary boundaries and the academic–practitioner divide". It is phenomenon-driven and not theory-driven, and deals with complex practical problems. It aims to bridge science, business and politics and again demonstrates the relational dimension (between disciplines and silos) of responsible leadership as a key variable in ensuring a sustainable future.

For transformative change towards a sustainable and equitable world, which McIntosh (2013) has termed "the necessary transition", responsible leadership must be developed both within disciplines, and across scientific and other types of disciplines altogether, including management, economic, political, social and natural sciences, legal disciplines and the humanities. Responsible leadership is needed in all areas of science to promote scientific understanding into business and governance systems that span the Earth. Similarly, responsible leadership is needed in business and global governance and political systems that take into consideration the new interdisciplinary imperatives being uncovered by basic and applied sciences. As I have argued, single discipline-based knowledge and leadership alone will be insufficient for humanity's "necessary transition" to a sustainable and equitable world.

Purpose of the conference

The purpose of the 3rd International Conference on Responsible Leadership was to create a forum where scholars of management and responsible leadership in business and government could come together with leading biological and physical scientists to generate shared perspectives and understanding across disciplinary boundaries. Many scientists are themselves attempting to bridge scientific disciplines, to create a dialogue about the multi-disciplinary insights needed to tackle increasingly complex issues such as genomics, disease, sustainability, energy and food security, to mention just a few. Each of these arenas is fraught with leadership responsibilities that are not bounded by the particular scientific disciplines but need to create bridges between what are now rather rigid boundaries, with little conversation going on among them. This conference brought together academics interested in

dialogue about the ethical, responsible, leadership and human implications of research within these complex and interconnected domains. *The Necessary Transition* (McIntosh, 2013) reflected transitions that are not only necessary but already in motion. In his keynote address during the conference, Professor Malcolm McIntosh added the following caveat, drawing on the work of Martin Rees, cosmologist and astrophysicist:

> What can we learn—or can we learn—from previous transitions in human history? In particular, what can be learnt from outside our disciplines? Global society depends precariously on elaborate networks—electricity grids, air-traffic control, international finance, just-in-time delivery, and so forth. Unless these are highly resilient, their manifest benefits could be outweighed by catastrophic (albeit rare) breakdowns, cascading through the system. [And] We are kidding ourselves if we think that those with technical expertise will all be balanced and rational.

As mentioned earlier in this editorial, science as such cannot be value-free. Personal interests more often than not compromise scientists and co-designers, and co-ownership of scientific progress is a rarity among them. Again, this is where I would like to advocate responsible leadership, its relational dimension and the potential it has for integration.

We need our leaders to be consultative, knowledgeable and wise. How can this be achieved given the current nature of siloed expertise? Waldman and Balven (2014) argue that we also need to acknowledge that responsible leadership introduces an important infliction point whereby the conflict between satisfying the concerns of owners on the one side, and broader stakeholders on the other, should form the basis of our investigations. This tension also applies to the siloed approach we find in business, politics and scientific innovation, and therefore I would like to add to this point by arguing for responsible leadership in science to emerge, where the role of social science finds its rightful place. It should follow an inclusive stakeholder approach where research is co-designed and owned by all participating stakeholders. In a symposium presented by Pearce *et al.* (2014), participants advocated a shared leadership approach as the key to responsible leadership.

In this special issue

In this special issue, we delve into the notion of responsibility, especially from the perspective of leadership. The five articles appearing in this edition offer multiple approaches and understandings of responsible leadership from diverse disciplinary perspectives. The authors have employed a variety of sources to facilitate dialogue between differing disciplines and interests to demonstrate the complexity of our attempts to describe responsible leadership.

Patricia Strong, in her paper entitled "Is integrated reporting a matter of public concern? Evidence from Australia", discusses the emergence of integrated reporting as a solution to the siloed reporting practices that place a distinction between compulsory financial/corporate reporting and voluntary sustainability reporting. Strong touches on reporting practices and illustrates a general trend that shows a lack of "ensuring accounting for sustainability impacts".

Strong presents integrated reporting as a practice congruous with responsible leadership in its accountability and transparency. Its complexity warrants its being a multidisciplinary endeavour—as leadership should be. Despite the rise of integrated reporting, she points out that very little research attention has been afforded to it. She also argues for further research in connecting responsible leadership with integrated reporting. Strong addresses this gap through her study, elucidating deeper and holistic insights into the underexplored field from an Australian standpoint.

Neil Eccles's paper entitled "Aiding and abetting an escape from disciplinary parochialism: A case study" argues that achieving a sustainable and equitable future (social justice) can be done through breaking down biases and disposing of disciplinary parochialism, which is the source of such biases. In essence, any responsible leader ought to work back to the initial cause (disciplinary parochialism) and effect a change in order to have a hope of achieving justice. To illustrate his argument, Eccles presents a case study based on a module presented to first-year economic and management sciences students. The study demonstrates how the module builds bridges with moral and political philosophy in order to initiate the process of breaking down parochialism.

In his paper entitled "Chief Mohlomi: A pioneer in bridging knowledge from enterprises of science, business and politics in southern Africa in the

18th century", Khali Mofuoa discusses Mosotho Chief Mohlomi and his style of leadership, which endeavoured to break from parochialism. He argues that the separation of fields/disciplines is the legacy of the 20th century phenomenon of specialization within the production of knowledge. In reality, however, life is not neatly compartmentalized into knowledge fields. This leads Mofuoa to argue that it is necessary to bridge this disciplinary/siloed gap; for this to be achieved, responsible leadership is needed. He is of the opinion that in a complex and interconnected world, leadership (and its inherent responsibilities) cannot be confined to consulting a single knowledge source. Khali also illustrates the importance of the link between the interdependent disciplines of science, business and politics, a synergy that facilitates steps towards ensuring sustainable development and fostering responsible leadership. Khali contextualizes the three disciplines in terms of Mohlomi's time and then propounds his argument for interdisciplinary dialogue by expounding on the seemingly successful practices of Mohlomi. In this paper Khali articulates his perception of the contextual relationship and intellectual relevance between our time and that of Mohlomi. He ends his argument by asserting, through Chief Mohlomi's example, that our world is interconnected and dealing with it requires dialogue between science, business and politics.

Joel Houdet and Claudious Chikozho approach the discourse on responsibility and responsible leadership from a different angle, focusing on our responsibility to the natural environment. In their paper entitled "The valuation of ecosystem services in South African environmental impact assessments: Review of selected mining case studies and implications for policy", the authors express the importance of being ecologically responsible. They do this by emphasizing the valuation of ecosystem services (such as food and water) and articulate the importance of being cognizant (as "governments, companies and citizens") of the benefits that are bestowed upon society as a whole by ecosystem services. Houdet and Chikozho argue that "economic agents" (such as businesses) usually take ecosystems and ecosystem services for granted. They posit that the "inability to understand" and "unwillingness to acknowledge" the nexus between economic agents' actions and their ecological impact lies at the heart of the problem. The authors illustrate their argument by using the mining industry as a microcosm of human beings' ecological impacts and the decisions that lead to them. They further argue for conclusively placing value on ecosystem services in order to better inform the decisions made by mining houses. The authors conclude by pointing out that valuation of ecosystem services needs careful consideration and that an integration of monetary and non-monetary values proffers a more comprehensive view (since they complement each other), as opposed to reliance upon one or the other.

Sope Williams-Elegbe, in her paper entitled "Citizens' response to irresponsible (or constrained) leadership as a catalyst for change: A critical assessment of leadership and followership in Nigeria", discusses the relationship between a responsible leader and a responsible follower within the context of democracy. It is assumed, Williams-Elegbe states, that democratic dispensation is congruous with (more) responsible leadership. This is not necessarily the case and Williams-Elegbe illustrates this with a critical analysis of "citizens' [followers] responses to the shortcomings of leadership in Nigeria". She further explains the pivotal role played by citizens in Nigeria in ensuring that the government remains accountable. Williams-Elegbe examines several instances of citizens' responses to government and the reaction of the government to any demands put forth by the citizens. She concludes by postulating that democracy is not a destination whose natural conclusion is more responsible leadership; rather, it is the departure point of a long journey. This speaks to the long journey of development in Nigeria which obligates both the government (leaders) and the citizens to play their respective roles as responsible individuals and organizations in a dynamic democracy.

The five papers included in this special edition and summarized above provide insight into responsible leadership and the importance of interdisciplinary dialogue in an interconnected and complex world. The perspectives are unique and disparate in a number of respects, yet they converge to give us focused insights on responsible leadership as an emerging discourse. They also confirm the importance of bridging science, business and politics, and the role that responsible leadership plays in this.

Finally, this editorial would argue for more active deliberation among academics on the level of analysis of leadership theory moving beyond the individual level to the collective level, bearing in mind multiple role-players and academic disciplines.

References

Bierman, F. (2007). Earth systems governance as a crosscutting theme of global change research. *Global Environmental Change*, 17 (3-4), 326-337.

Crompton, T. (2010). *Common Cause: The case for working with our cultural values*. England: World Wildlife Fund-UK.

Dionne, D.S., Gupta, A., Sotak, K.L., Shirrefs, K.A., Serban, A., Hao, C., Kim, H.H., & Yammarino, F.J. (2014). A 25-year perspective on levels of analysis in leadership research. *Leadership Quarterly*, 25, 6-35.

The Economist (2015, September 26). The Volkswagen Scandal. A mucky business. *The Economist*. Retrieved from http://www.economist.com/news/briefing/21667918-systematic-fraud-worlds-biggest-carmaker-threatens-engulf-entire-industry-and.

Freeman, E., & Auster, R. (2011). Values, authenticity and responsible leadership. *Journal of Business Ethics*, 98, 15-23.

Maak, T. & Pless, N. (2006). Responsible leadership in a stakeholder society: A relational perspective. *Journal of Business Ethics*, 66, 99-115.

McIntosh, M. (2013). *The Necessary Transition: The Journey towards the Sustainable Enterprise Economy*. Sheffield: Greenleaf Publishing.

Mervis, P., De Jongh, D., Googins, B., Quinn, L., & Van Velsor, E. (2010). *Responsible Leadership Emerging: Individual, Organizational and Collective Frontiers*. Pretoria: Albert Luthuli Centre for Responsible Leadership, University of Pretoria.

Pearce, C.L., Wassenaar, C.L., & Manz, C.C. (2014). Is shared leadership the key to responsible leadership? *Academy of Management Perspectives*, 28(3).

Shrivastava, P., Ivanaj, S., & Persson, S. (2013). Transdisciplinary study of sustainable enterprises. *Business Strategy and the Environment*, 22(4), 230-244.

Stahl, G.K., & De Luque, M.S. (2014). Antecedents of responsible leader behavior: A research synthesis, conceptual framework, and agenda for future research. *Academy of Management Perspectives*, 28(3).

Voegtlin, C. (2015). What does it mean to be responsible? Addressing the missing responsibility dimension in ethical leadership research. *Leadership*. 2 April. doi 10.1177/1742715015578936, 1-29.

Voegtlin, C., & Scherer, A.G. (2014). Responsible innovation and the innovation of responsibility: Governing sustainable development in a globalized world. *Journal of Business Ethics*. 12 September. doi 10.1007/s10551-015-2769-z.

Waldman, D.A., & Balven, R.M. (2014). Responsible leadership: Theoretical issues and research directions. *Academy of Management Perspectives*, 28(3).

Young, I.M. (2011). *Responsibility for Justice*. Oxford: Oxford University Press.

Professor **Derick de Jongh** is the Founding Director of the Albert Luthuli Centre for Responsible Leadership at the University of Pretoria. Prior to joining the University of Pretoria, he founded the Centre for Corporate Citizenship at the University of South Africa.

✉ The Albert Luthuli Centre for Responsible Leadership, Department of Business Management, Faculty of Economic and Management Sciences, University of Pretoria, South Africa

🖥 Derick.dejongh@up.ac.za

The Journal of Corporate Citizenship Issue 60 *December 2015* © Greenleaf Publishing 2015

DOI: [10.9774/GLEAF.4700.2015.de.00004]

Seeking Sustainability Leadership

Jem Bendell and Richard Little, FRGS, FCIPD, MBPS

University of Cumbria, UK

This paper critiques mainstream leadership and leadership development approaches to help inform the emerging field of sustainability leadership. Traditional leadership theory and education is argued to be highly problematic for the pursuit of sustainability leadership. A more critical approach is required, drawing upon insights from social theory, critical discourse analysis and psychology, which is attempted in this paper. Once deconstructed, leadership can be a useful framework for exploring needed learning and unlearning for people to become agents within leaderful groups to create more significant change in organizations and society, in light of unsustainability and injustice. The initial outlines of a reconstructed approach to leadership and its development, which are used at the Institute for Leadership and Sustainability (IFLAS) and Impact International, are outlined.

- Leadership
- Leadership development
- Sustainability leadership
- Sustainable leadership
- Critical leadership
- Critical management

Jem Bendell is a Professor of Sustainability Leadership and Founding Director of the Institute for Leadership and Sustainability (IFLAS) at the University of Cumbria in the United Kingdom, which runs the world's largest specialist sustainability MBA programme. He has over 20 years of experience in responsible business, sustainable development, transformative philanthropy and sustainable currencies. With over 100 publications, including UN reports and four books, in 2007 he co-wrote the WWF report *Deeper Luxury* on the social and environmental performance of luxury brands. In 2012 the World Economic Forum appointed him a Young Global Leader, in recognition of his promotion of alliances for sustainable development.

University of Cumbria, Charlotte Mason Building, Rydal Road, Ambleside, LA22 9BB, UK

jem.bendell@cumbria.ac.uk

Richard is an Associate Scholar at the Institute for Leadership and Sustainability (IFLAS) and an external lecturer at the University of Cumbria, delivering post-graduate modules on experiential education, facilitation, leadership, democracy and dialogue. He is a leadership specialist with Impact International and leader of a 10 year programme to develop senior academic and research leadership at a major research university. For 30 years he has undertaken multiple professional activities in Japan and Singapore advising on questions of public service leadership.

Impact International, Cragwood House, Windermere, Cumbria, LA23 1LQ, UK

richard.little@cumbria.ac.uk

> There are two types of education... One should teach us how to make a living, and the other how to live (John Adams, 1780).

> Democracy has to be born anew every generation, and education is its midwife (John Dewey, 1916).

A S PEOPLE WHO HAVE WORKED for some decades to help a fundamental shift in capitalism for a more sustainable and fair economy, we were somewhat relieved to hear more executives acknowledge that the current efforts are not enough. According to Accenture and the UN Global Compact, only a third of CEOs of the world's 1,000 largest firms think that business is making sufficient efforts to address global sustainability challenges or that the global economy is on track to meet growing demands for employment and consumption (Accenture, 2013). Take any major issue, and the innovations at firm level are dwarfed by data on deteriorating circumstances. For instance, we might be encouraged that solar power will soon be cheaper than coal, but harrowed by how aggregate carbon emissions rise every year (IPCC, 2014).

This growing realization that incremental change might be insignificant change may be one reason why we now hear calls for more leadership for sustainability (Adams *et al.*, 2011). One study found over 50 new sustainability leadership courses, in English, around the world: "colleges and universities are rushing to respond to an increasingly urgent challenge: developing the next generation of sustainability leaders" (Shriberg and MacDonald, 2013, p 1). The international Academy for Business in Society's conference in 2014 focused on "Leadership for a Sustainable Future". Hosted at the University of Cambridge's Institute for Sustainability Leadership (CISL), the organizers noted that "progress may well depend on the emergence of political, economic and intellectual leadership far beyond what is currently in evidence" (ABIS, 2014a). The director of CISL went further, stating "If companies stand any chance of meaningfully embedding sustainability policies and principles into business practices and performance, they must invest in integrating sustainability into their mainstream leadership and management development programmes" (Courtice, 2014).

So the search for sustainability leadership is now on. Where will this leadership come from? What will it look like? How can we see more of it? Our experience is that people are calling for more leadership without reflecting on what leadership means, and also, when they do, too often relying on mainstream management discourses about leadership. This is reflected in research of sustainability leadership programmes, where their "directors, most of whom have a sustainability background but not a leadership background, had difficulty answering the question of how their programs differed from traditional leadership programs" (Shriberg and MacDonald, 2013, p 12). Our argument is that as educators and researchers in fields related to sustainability, we should not simply seek to add more sustainability to leadership or add more leadership to sustainability, but challenge assumptions about "leadership" that have added to the persistent social and environmental problems we experience today.

In this paper we briefly outline the importance of the field of leadership education, before defining our focus as leadership behaviours, rather than individual leaders with senior roles. We understand leadership as a relational, "socially constructed" phenomenon rather than the result of a stable set of leadership attributes that inhere in "leaders" (Wood, 2005). We will describe the growth of "sustainability leadership" as a topic in the field of business–society relations and its associated research community, as well as a topic for increasing numbers of degree programmes around the world. We will describe some of the major shortcomings of the approaches to leadership and its development which are currently mainstream within business schools, and why that is so, before outlining a more critical approach. We conclude by presenting a couple of the orientations that we aim to cultivate in participants in our leadership development programmes. In so doing, we hope to inform discussions on the future development of research, advice and education on sustainability leadership.

Leadership and its development

Leadership is a subject offered in most business schools worldwide as well as a variety of management trainers. The focus of these courses is often on personal development to prepare oneself for greater seniority within an organization, which makes it attractive to many students and educators. The popularity of the field is reflected by the University of Cumbria asking one of your authors in 2012 to found an Institute for Leadership and Sustainability (IFLAS). The subject has a range of journals dedicated to it, including *Leadership, The Leadership Quarterly* and *Journal of Leadership Studies*, as well as being a subject often covered in journals like *Organisation* or *Human Relations*. Recently, articles have examined the growing field of leadership development courses offered to executives. "One estimate cites a $45 billion annual expenditure in the United States alone for leadership development and a survey of European CEOs found that the majority were 'extremely' committed to leadership development" (Gagnon and Collinson, 2014, p. 648). Mabey and Finch-Lees (2008) found that leadership development programmes comprise a "potent and high-profile human resources activity, involving some of the organization's key players and attracting high investment both in terms of corporate budgets and expectations" (p. 3).

There are so many definitions of leadership, which makes it hard to pick one, so we will offer one of our own: Leadership is any behaviour that has the effect of helping groups of people achieve something that the majority of them are pleased with and which we assess as significant and what they would not have otherwise achieved. Therefore leadership involves the ascription of significance to an act by us, the observer, where significance usually involves our assumptions or propositions about values and theories of change. If our theory of change is that the CEO has freedom of action and can impose change, then we would naturally look for leadership to be exhibited at that level. If our values are that profit-maximizing for shareholders in the near term is a good goal, then we would not question a CEO's "leadership" if achieving such goals. We should note that these are rather big "Ifs".

In the same way it is us the observer that attributes "leadership" to a behaviour that we observe, rather than a behaviour having an intrinsic quality that we happen to call leadership, so it is the same with recognizing a "leader". We might see someone as a "leader" when we perceive they have done something to help others do useful and significant things that they would not have done otherwise. But does this mean we are assuming that "leader" is a stable characteristic of a person? Perhaps something intrinsic to them? Both leadership and leader are our own narratives about a self, rather than something real in the world independent of our descriptions. As Gergen (1994) explained well, "narratives of the self are not personal impulses made social, but social processes realised on the site of the personal". The truth about leaders and leadership are not things to be discovered, but processes of social construction, and reflect our own discourses and preoccupations at any given time. By virtue of nature, nurture or circumstance, some people are better suited to certain activities than others, but the labelling of such actions as leadership and such people as leaders is dependent on what we are choosing to mean by such terms and choosing to recognize and ignore in any situation.

Sustainability meets leadership

The process of social construction in the field of leadership has been a creative one, often lucrative, with now at least a hundred adjectives added to leadership to describe individual intentions, the behaviours involved, or the nature of the outcomes. Some of the more interesting adjectives that have sparked great followings are Servant, Democratic, Authentic, Situational and Transformational.

Leadership is increasingly prefixed by the word "sustainability". Usually when discussing sustainability leadership, people focus on the stated goal of the leadership or the outcome, which relates to varying conceptions of sustainable development, or greater resilience in the face of environmental disruptions. Less so at present do people focus on the behaviours during leadership, such as the ethical frameworks involved or the embodied values (was she wearing an ethically made suit when she fired the staff?). A definition of sustainability leadership that builds on the earlier definition of leadership, and encompasses intention, act and outcome, while delaying disputes on the nature of sustainable development, could be as follows:

> Sustainability leadership is any ethical behaviour that has the intention and effect of helping groups of people achieve environmental or social outcomes that we assess as significant and that they would not have otherwise achieved.

Recent analysis of sustainability leadership has listed both traits and competencies that individual leaders need to exhibit. One of the few academic studies on sustainability leadership describes a rather large task:

> Leadership for sustainability requires leaders of extraordinary abilities. These are leaders who can read and predict through complexity, think through complex problems, engage groups in dynamic adaptive organisational change and have the emotional intelligence to adaptively engage with their own emotions associated with complex problem solving (Metcalf and Benn 2013).

This analysis implies we need more remarkable individuals to turn the tide of unsustainability. Although this could imply we need lots of clever people to apply themselves to the problem, such an analysis can have the opposite effect, of emphasizing the role of exceptional individual leaders at the expense of collective, collaborative and democratic efforts. Leadership, we would argue, is a necessary function in such efforts, but as an enabling, distributed form of action.

The University of Cambridge conducted a study of leadership development programmes from a perspective that analyzed them for their implications for greater organizational sustainability.

> Very few of the companies we interviewed had achieved integration of sustainability into the curriculum design of their formal executive development programmes. And even in the few instances where this was the case, the inclusion of sustainability tended to be rather reactive, in the form of bolt-on modules or sessions—the sustainability director or by an outside speaker—rather than an integrated theme that permeated the whole development process and reflected the world-view of the company and the top leadership vision (Courtice, 2014).

After attending or analysing a number of leadership development courses offered by top business schools, we have experienced similar limitations, and worse. Most courses are a mix of content from academics from across disciplines that are available to the course director, some "old males tales" about insights gained from a high-level career, some uncritical and rather boring case studies of "successful" CEOs or entrepreneurs, and finally some group discussions on leadership that draw from the latest popular leadership theories, without any critical deconstruction of them. After analysing these courses and their leadership texts, we have come to the view that mainstream corporate and academic assumptions about leadership are fundamentally flawed and sustainability professionals should not accept them uncontested. Therefore, for projects that seek to add more sustainability to leadership development (Rogan and DeCew, 2014) or "identify barriers to and opportunities for the integration of sustainability into corporate leadership training and development programmes" (ABIS, 2014b) there is a need to challenge the most basic assumptions of what leadership is and how it can be developed. Otherwise, a focus on integrating sustainability into leadership development could create unfounded delusions of how one can encourage organizational and sectoral change towards social or environmental goals. We realize these may seem bold statements, and so we will now explain what some of the failings of mainstream leadership discourses are, and the implications for taking a different approach.

The un-sustainability of leadership

One of the characteristics of mainstream leadership discussion is an implicit hero-focus. Most popular literature on leadership and most leadership development addresses individuals in senior roles, as if only senior leaders exhibit leadership, and as if their leadership is always a key factor shaping outcomes. Psychological research since the 1980s has demonstrated that people, across cultures, tend to over-attribute significance to the actions of senior leaders, when compared to other factors shaping outcomes (Meindl *et al.*, 1985). The researchers concluded that this was evidence that we are susceptible to seeing "leadership" when it isn't necessarily there or important—a collectively constructed "romantic discourse". Their work reflects the "false attribution effect", widely reported by social psychologists, as people's tendency to place an undue emphasis on internal characteristics to explain someone's behaviour, rather than considering external factors (Jones and Harris, 1967). Perhaps our particular susceptibility to this effect when considering leadership is because we are brought up with stories of great leaders shaping history (it is easier to tell stories that way), and this myth is perpetuated by our business media today. Every business magazine applauds their heroes. For instance, in 1996, Jeff Skilling was described in a *Fortune* magazine article as, "the most intellectually brilliant executive in the natural-gas business" and received years of praise for his leadership of Enron from that magazine, before serving time in a Chicago jail for fraud at the company (Brady, 2010).

This over-attribution of importance to a "leader" is an obstacle to our understanding change towards sustainability, as it can curtail our analysis of why situations exist, and it undermines the potential of that vast majority without senior roles, as the implication is that they can't shape outcomes. The way we over attribute importance to leaders also means we ignore that leadership is context-dependent rather than a fixed quality and behaviour of an individual. Our boss may be good at some things in some situations, but leadership can usefully be thought of as emergent, distributed and episodic, with different people contributing at different times (Raelin, 2003; Starhawk, 1987). These are reasons why Gemmil and Oakley (2011) argue:

> Leadership is a myth that functions to reinforce existing social beliefs and structures about the necessity of hierarchy and leaders in organizations ... a serious sign of social pathology, a special case of a myth that induces massive learned helplessness among members of a social system.

This obsession with a special boss leads to the second approach to leadership analysis that is important to avoid—the desired traits, or personality characteristics, of a leader. Try an internet news search for leader traits and the popularity of this approach will be instantly apparent. Yet it is flawed as most of the traits identified as key for leaders, such as empathy or self-efficacy, are key for anyone who is remotely capable. In addition, we aren't fixed beings but act in different ways in different contexts and change over time. The damaging consequence of a focus on traits is that it suggests some are born to be the boss of a hierarchy and need to be selected to do so, rather than consider what forms of hierarchy or non-hierarchy can elicit the best group behaviours to achieve desired goals.

Another main focus in mainstream leadership development is self-justification, which often masquerades as self-exploration. The current popularity of "Authentic Leadership" reflects this approach, where executives are encouraged to seek coherence between their life story and seeking or holding a senior role in a corporation (George et al., 2007). The potential benefits are more self-confidence, appearing more authentic in one's job, and enhanced skills of public oratory. Rather than self-exploration, these processes can be characterized as a process of self-justification, as the exploration of self is framed by the aim of constructing narratives that explain one's right to seniority within a corporation—an almost "divine" right to lead. Having participated in such processes, we did not find encouragement for self-realizations that might undermine one's ability to work for certain firms, or transform the basis of one's self-worth, or challenge one's assumption of self-efficacy.

This approach ignores insights from critical sociology that shows how our perspectives and sense of self are shaped by language and discourse, operating through mass media and various forms of social communication (Fairclough, 1989). Such insights challenge the view that we can achieve depths of "self-awareness" through only reflecting on our experiences and feelings without the input of different social theories. If your analysis is that unsustainability is a product of our existing social norms and economic structures, then helping each other free ourselves from mainstream delusions about reality and success must be a starting point for any self-leadership. The practices of "Authentic Leadership" development are similar to those used in the broader field of "transformational leadership" where leaders are regarded as charismatic individuals who create change in organizations to achieve higher purposes (Bass and Steidlmeier, 1999).

We are not arguing that there is no place for authentic or transformational leadership development. In some cases, particularly for those lacking self-confidence or coming from disadvantaged communities, there are benefits from developing self-efficacy in typical ways. However, the focus on heroic leadership, key traits, and self-justification in much leadership development within business schools arises due to the assumption that captains of industry must control, rather than liberate, normal people and nature. That is the "managerialist" mind-set that identifies "us", the bosses, as people who need to manage "them", the unruly masses, to achieve goals, rather than celebrate and coach our participation in the evolving multitude of life. It is a mind-set descended from the so-called "scientific management" that emerged in the 1940s and treats staff like mechanical parts (Rost, 1997). It is a mind-set that is causing us to alienate ourselves from nature and each other, and therefore is a mind-set at the root of unsustainability (Eisenstein, 2013).

Our view is that mainstream leadership concepts and education are flawed due to reflecting a confluence, in the West, of three great 20th century flows: first, scientific management and the perfection of panoptic managerialism; second, an addiction to fantasies of individual potency and a corresponding distrust, notwithstanding democratic rhetoric, of collaborative, collective forms of deliberation, problem-solving and organization; and third, the monetization of every kind of human activity or exchange in a crudely delineated market that displaces democratic social choice. In their mingling, the three form a near-impregnable "common-sense", which is often voiced in what Giacalone and Politslo (2013) call "econophonic" language (where financial calculation dominates) and "potensiphonic" language (where the emphasis is on individual power). This voice tells us—with typical phrases such as "at the end of the day, when push comes to shove, in the real world"—that without strong leadership, nothing will ever get done. From that perspective "strong" leadership is assumed to be the opposite of something weak and equivocal that might involve collective deliberation and argument in the public sphere. With these assumptions underpinning corporate cultures it is less surprising that psychologists find there to be an above-average rate of people with psychopathic tendencies in corporate executive roles (Bendell, 2002).

A search for sustainability leadership and its development can begin by setting aside these dominant assumptions about strength as well as the idea of the senior leader, to consider leadership as something shared, an episodic social process for participation in which we can all become competent. Therefore we do not agree with those who argue for building upon existing leadership theories like transformational leadership (Shriberg and MacDonald, 2013), unless that is done with a critical perspective and experimental method.

Seeking sustainability leadership along other paths

Our arguments on sustainability leadership build upon a range of scholarship that is coming to be known as 'Critical Leadership Studies', which critiques mainstream assumptions, in society and in academia, of what leadership involves. Such scholarship addresses the social and political effects of socially constructed notions and practices of leadership, to the "romance of leadership" whereby magical thinking about leaders may infantilize people while creating a strong illusion of empowerment and to leadership as a gendered practice and to the development of leadership as "identity work" that shapes people's sense of their organizational roles (Birkeland, 1993). By "critical leadership", we do not mean, like Jenkins (2012), the application of systematic logical thought by senior role holders. Rather, we draw upon the sociological understanding of "critical" as involving the deconstruction of widespread discourses and assumptions that are maintained by, and perpetuate, certain power relations (Sutherland et al., 2014).

Fortunately for the development of sustainability leadership, practical implications from Critical Leadership Studies can be developed and applied in leadership development. In addition, important examples of different forms of leadership are found in some environmental organizations (Egri and Herman, 2000), activist communities (Sutherland et al., 2014), and are exhibited by some senior executives. The late Ray Anderson, when he was CEO of Interface, exhibited a different approach to sustainability leadership to that widely taught today. In a gathering organized by Impact International he explained how he appreciated that the goal of transforming the company towards zero emissions would be something that all employees would be inspired by when recognizing it was about their own families and communities. He knew that the existing hierarchies and systems would likely restrict their efforts to achieve that goal. He knew the vision would be compelling and colleagues would discover how to achieve it, because "we weren't making carpet tiles any more, we were transforming industry and commerce". "Management was likely to be the biggest obstacle" he said. "It was down to me to make sure that nothing would prevent people taking this on and using their imaginations" (Anderson, 2007).

There are many other business leaders we can learn from, yet many of the leadership behaviours that need to be cultivated will be found outside the C-suite and also outside the corporate sector altogether, in non-profits, social enterprises, cooperatives and activist networks (Sutherland et al., 2014). For instance, some non-profit environmental leaders have been found to espouse and practise personal values that are more "ecocentric, open to change, and self-transcendent" than business managers (Egri and Herman, 2000). Future research on sustainability leadership and how to develop it could usefully focus on non-corporate leadership behaviours and seek to integrate these with general leadership development.

On the basis of a critical deconstruction of leadership discourses, our assessment of what is useful for organizational change, and an awareness of the imperatives of wider sustainability, social justice and personal dignity, we have identified 12 key "orientations" that we seek to promote among participants of our leadership development courses and coaching. We call them orientations rather than attributes, competencies or capabilities, as they describe areas for ongoing attention and evolution, rather than achieving a level of performance. This Turning Point article is not the place to explore all these orientations, but we want to describe for you two of them that relate to the limitations of mainstream leadership that we described above.

Instead of a focus on heroes with great traits, to develop sustainability leadership we can enhance our understanding of how to develop leaderful groups, where senior role holders act as hosts not heroes, and enable leadership to emerge from within the group (Raelin, 2003). We call this orientation "group literacy". It arises from a desire to help a group better serve a social purpose, understanding why groups malfunction and what forms of intervention can help them function better.

For this kind of leadership we can gain useful insights from how professional facilitators work to help groups function well. Some analysis suggests that groups malfunction due to misunderstandings of, or lack of attention to, either meaning, values or structure (Heron, 1999). Problems in the domain of meaning include a sense of purposelessness, confusion, with unclear or disputed goals, "goal displacement", untested assumptions, and misunderstandings.

Problems in the domain of values can generate alienation, exclusion, pessimism, disrespect, cultural misunderstanding, domination or dependency, and disengagement. Problems in the domain of structure can involve a structure–task mismatch, role confusion, secrecy, unnecessary bureaucracy, lack of resources, no timelines or milestones, or too many. Leadership can therefore involve participants in a group noticing which domain is in need of attention, and stepping up to seek to address that, and then stepping back when that particular task is done. "Group literacy" requires knowing what good facilitation is, and helping that function occur within the group, while conscious of the limitations that arise for one if taking on such a role. Another aspect of this approach is to encourage assessment of how a group is functioning as an organ of leadership, both of itself and a wider group of stakeholders. Groups may appear leaderless to some observers but achieve leadership of themselves and others (Sutherland *et al.*, 2014).

A second orientation that we seek to cultivate is "self-construal". Instead of processes of self-exploration being managed towards self-justification, we encourage deeper self-construal where no outcome is hoped for. As one recent student on the Post Graduate Certificate in Sustainable Leadership explained to us, her tutors, we offered "an existential provocation demanding full emotional engagement within a democratic and nurturing community". Enabling this type of self-exploration involves insights from critical sociology, psychology, philosophy and spiritual traditions, as well as deep conversations, group work and experiences in nature. Such exploration must be done responsibly, sensitive to the participant's willingness to explore.

The almost required optimism of a sustainability profession seeking favour with mainstream economic powers can be a barrier to engaging in this form of leadership development, because it does not provide space to explore insights that might prove difficult to existing institutions, discourses and income streams. Another barrier to a depth of reflection is the widespread denial that recent climate science might imply it is too late to avoid abrupt climate change (Foster, 2014). In our experience, many professionals are wedded to the idea of progress, and that at personal and collective levels we are "moving forward". This is also true with people working on sustainability. Yet being able to allow a sense of despair at a lack of progress, or any progress as traditionally conceived, is important to allow true self-exploration that might involve letting go of past assumptions about oneself and society. It is about moving from a leadership as desperate heroes to divine hosts. We use the word divine, as ultimately a discussion of leadership becomes one of purpose, which makes it an issue involving the deepest questions facing us, the meaning of our lives, our species, and the cosmic plan or comic fluke we call planet Earth.

Despite our criticisms of the assumptions and approaches of "authentic leadership" and "transformational leadership", the focus on self-development within these mainstream leadership development practices provides an opening for work on the deeper personal transformations that might enable more leadership for sustainability. In addition, the question of purpose is now receiving greater attention from leadership scholars, without that purpose being assumed to be congruent with narrowly defined corporate goals (Kempster *et al.*, 2011). To be useful for sustainability, we believe leadership development needs to avoid the seductive construction of self-efficacy within an assumed and pro-gressing cultural and economic system. Instead, educators can reconnect with the timeless essence of education as enabling greater freedom (Dewey, 1916), and thus focus on encouraging students to openly and critically explore notions of self and society. Brazilian teacher Paulo Freire (1970) wrote that education is either an exercise in domestication or liberation. If as educators we have come to the understanding that current paradigms of thought in economy and society are fundamentally inhibiting our ability to live in more sustainable ways, then education for liberation is a key part of developing leadership for sustainability (Bendell, 2014).

The growing backlash against mainstream university courses from some successful entrepreneurs, such as Peter Thiel (2014), could be due to a lack of both critical and empowering education at many universities today. The enterprise-oriented training that he and other entrepreneurs advocate will be unlikely to enable shifts in consciousness that we are seeing in participants in our courses and so we see an important and wonderful role for universities in years to come if more academics embrace their unique role. To help, we will continue to document and share the 12 orientations that we seek to promote through our leadership education, as well as the future results from evaluations of graduate performance, where participants invite colleagues to anonymously assess them before and after the course.

Conclusions

In this paper we have critiqued mainstream leadership and leadership develop-ment approaches in the hope of better grounding the emerging field of sus-tainability leadership. "Sustainability leadership cannot be taught solely with traditional leadership theory" argue Shriberg and MacDonald (2013, p. 18). In this paper, we have gone further, by arguing that traditional leadership theory is highly problematic to the pursuit of sustainability leadership. Their study of sustainability leadership programmes found that "this emerging area suf-fers from a lack of common frameworks, methods and metrics" (Shriberg and MacDonald, 2013, p 17). We agree that more learning between practitioners in sustainability leadership development is important, and our paper contributes in making clear some problems with existing mainstream approaches to lead-ership. Without a critical view on leadership, the emerging area of incorporat-ing sustainability into existing leadership development might repeat the same mistake that had led to sustainable business efforts being largely ineffectual in changing the direction of our economies. That mistake was trying to incorporate sustainability into the mainstream, rather than analysing and transforming those aspects of the mainstream that are driving mal-development (Bendell and Doyle, 2014).

We hope, with Courtice (2014) of CISL, that:

> as sustainability becomes more strategic, we expect mainstream leadership development programmes to change quite radically: to become more proactive (rather than responsive) and to put the individual's development into a much richer global context shaped by social and environmental trends and emerging norms.

However, this should not mean accepting the discourses of leadership that currently dominate.

After years of educating executives on sustainability leadership, it is our conviction that neither seeking to add leadership to sustainability practice or more sustainability to leadership practice is sufficient, because that could reinforce a set of ideas about leadership that are part of a corporate system that has contributed to social and environmental malaise. Instead, we can draw upon critical perspectives on leadership to dismantle unhelpful ideologies of hierarchy and power, and empower far more people to exhibit leadership for sustainability in many ways and at many levels.

Therefore our search for sustainability leadership must begin with unlearning leadership as it is currently assumed and most often taught. Templates for sustainability leadership won't be found within the walls of schools focused on corporate elites. Instead, we can widen our search to include critical sociology, deeper psychological reflection and inspiration from wild nature. The challenge for professionals in sustainability and corporate responsibility, therefore, is now to move beyond their existing expertise in social or environmental content, and explore the fundamentals of leadership and its development from a critical perspective.

References

ABIS (2014a) ABIS Annual Colloquium 2014 Transforming Tomorrow: Leadership for a Sustainable Future, Conference Website, http://www.abis-global.org/events/colloquium-2014. Accessed January 11th 2014.

ABIS (2014b) Leadership and Sustainability, Conference Website, http://www.abis-global.org/projects/leadership-and-sustainability. Accessed January 11th 2014.

Adams, J. (1780). Letter to Abigail Adams, May 12, 1780. http://www.john-adams-heritage.com/quotes/. Accessed January 11th 2014.

Adams, C.A., Heijltjes M.H., Jack G., Marjoribanks T. and Powell M. (2011). The development of leaders able to respond to climate change and sustainability challenges: The role of business schools, in *Sustainability Accounting, Management and Policy Journal*, Volume 2, Issue 1.

Bass, B. M. & Steidlmeier, P. (1999). Ethics, character, and authentic transformational leadership behaviour, *Leadership Quarterly*, Volume 10, Number 2, pp 181-217.

Bendell, J. (2002) Psychos in suits: corporate CEOs in need of (an) asylum, Open Democracy, 23 July 2002. https://www.opendemocracy.net/theme_7-corporations/article_260.jsp

Bendell, J. (2014) *Exploring Sustainability, Inaugural Professorial Lecture*, Words By the Water Festival, March 14th 2014, Keswick, UK. https://www.youtube.com/watch?v=j-Opqi-2UgY

Bendell, J. & Doyle, I. (2014). *Healing Capitalism*. Greenleaf Publishing: Sheffield, UK.

Birkeland, J. (1993). Ecofeminism: Linking Theory and Practice, in Gaard, G. (Ed.) Ecofeminism. Temple University Press: Philadelphia, USA.

Brady, C. (2010). An unlikely inspiration: Enron's Jeff Skilling, *Financial Times*, December 6. http://www.ft.com/intl/cms/s/2/078b7dfc-fdff-11df-853b-00144feab49a.html#axzz3OQVHqJr6. Accessed January 11th 2014.

Dewey, J. (1916). *Democracy and Education: An Introduction to the Philosophy of Education*. The Macmillan Company (reprint 1930). https://archive.org/stream/democracyand educoodeweuoft#page/n5/mode/2up

Egri, C. P. & Herman, S. (2000). 'Leadership in the North American environmental sector: Values, leadership styles, and contexts of environmental leaders and their organizations, *The Academy of Management Journal*, Volume 43, No. 4, pp 571-604.

Eisenstein, C. (2013). *The More Beautiful World Our Hearts Know is Possible*, Sacred Activism Books: USA.

Fairclough, N. (1989). *Language and Power*. Longman: Harlow, UK.

Freire, P. (1970). Pedagogy of the Oppressed, translated by Myra Ramos. Continuum: New York. http://www.pedagogyoftheoppressed.com/about/

George, B. et al (2007). Discovering your authentic leadership, *Harvard Business Review*, Volume 85, No. 2, February, pp 129-138.

Kempster, S. et al (2011). Leadership as purpose: exploring the role of purpose in leadership practice, *Leadership*, Volume 7, No. 3, pp. 317-334.

Gagnon, S. & Collinson, D. (2014). Rethinking global leadership development programmes: the interrelated significance of power, context and identity, *Organization Studies*, Volume 35, pp 645.

Gemmil, G. & Oakley, J. (2011). Leadership, an alienating social myth, *Human Relations*, Volume 45, Issue 2.

Gergen, K.J. (1994). *Realities and relationships: Soundings in social construction*. Cambridge, Massachusetts, and London, England: Harvard University Press.

Giacalone, R.A. & Promislo, M.D. (2013). Broken when entering: the stigmatization of goodness and business ethics education, *Academy of Management Learning & Education*, Vol. 12, No. 1.

Heron, J. (1999). *The Complete Facilitator's Handbook*, Kogan Page Ltd.

IPCC (2014). *The Fifth Assessment Report (AR5) of the United Nations Intergovernmental Panel on Climate Change (IPCC)*. http://www.ipcc.ch/report/ar5/index.shtml.

Jones, E.E., & Harris, V.A. (1967). The attribution of attitudes, *Journal of Experimental Social Psychology*, Volume 3, Issue 1 pp 1–24.

Jenkins, D. (2012). Global critical leadership: educating global leaders with critical leadership competencies, *Journal of Leadership Studies*, Volume 6, Number 2.

Mabey, C. & Finch-Lees, T. (2008). *Management and leadership development*. London: SAGE Publications.

Meindl, J. R., Ehrlich, S. B. & Dukerich, J. M. (1985). The romance of leadership, *Administrative Science Quarterly*, Volume 30, pp 78-102.

Metcalf, L. & Benn, S. (2013). Leadership for sustainability: an evolution of leadership ability, *Journal of Business Ethics*, February 2013, Volume 112, Issue 3, pp 369-384. http://link.springer.com/article/10.1007/s10551-012-1278-6

Raelin, J. A. (2003). *Creating Leaderful Organizations: How to Bring out Leadership in Everyone*. San Francisco: Berrett-Koehler.

Rogan, J. & DeCew, S. (2014). *Highlights from the GNAM Faculty Week on Sustainability Leadership*, http://som.yale.edu/highlights-gnam-faculty-week-sustainability-leadership?blog=3490. Accessed January 11th 2014.

Rost, J.C. (1997). Moving from individual to relationship: A postindustrial paradigm of leadership, *The Journal of Leadership Studies*, Volume 4, Issue 4, pp. 3-16.

Shriberg, M. & MacDonald, L. (2013). Sustainability leadership programs: emerging goals, methods & best practices, *Journal of Sustainability Education*, Volume 5, May 2013.

Sutherland, N. et al (2014). Anti-leaders(hip) in social movement organizations: the case of autonomous grassroots groups, in *Organization*, November 2014, Volume 21, pp 759-781.

Starhawk (1987). *Truth or Dare: Encounters with Power, Authority and Mystery*. San Francisco, Harper and Row.

Thiel, P. (2014). Zero to One: Notes on Start-Ups or How to Build the Future. Crown Business, USA.

Wood, M. (2005). The fallacy of misplaced leadership, *Journal of Management Studies*, Volume 42, No. 6 pp 1101–121.

DOI: [10.9774/GLEAF.4700.2015.de.00005]

Citizens' Response to Irresponsible (or Constrained) Leadership as a Catalyst for Change

A Critical Assessment of Leadership and Followership in Nigeria

Sope Williams-Elegbe
Stellenbosch University, South Africa

Many countries in sub-Saharan Africa have enjoyed a political and economic renaissance in the last 25 years. It is generally assumed that a stable democracy is synonymous with responsible (or at least, more responsible) leadership, howsoever defined. One country that appears to deny this assumption is Nigeria. An assessment of responsible leadership indicators against the types of leadership that Nigeria has endured since the return to a democratic form of government in 1999, illustrates that the Nigerian democracy does not appear to be attracting the kind of leadership that can translate political rhetoric into developmental benefits. There are several reasons for this, which include: the educational constraints present in Nigeria; the vestiges of military governance, which has limited the collective awareness of appropriate leadership styles; and the funding mechanism for political office, which excludes the intelligentsia and the middle class from effectively participating in the political process, among others. This paper presents a critical assessment of citizens' responses to the shortcomings of leadership in Nigeria. It will examine for instance: civil society initiatives; next-generation activism; and (social) media responses to leadership failings in Nigeria between 1999 and 2014. The paper will conclude with an assessment of citizen-led measures and their success and an examination of whether these citizen-led measures affected the quality and nature of leadership in Nigeria.

- Leadership
- Social change
- Social media
- Citizen activism
- Nigeria

Sope Williams-Elegbe holds an LLB (Lagos), LLM (London School of Economics), and PhD (Nottingham). She is a Senior Lecturer in Law at the University of Lagos, Nigeria and a Research Fellow and Deputy Director of the African Public Procurement Regulation Research Unit, Stellenbosch University, South Africa.

sopewe@sun.ac.za; www.sun.ac.za

DEMOCRACY IN NIGERIA HAS FAILED to translate to good governance and effective leadership. Cases of corruption and nepotism still plague the country's governance structures despite the end of a military-led dictatorial system of governance in 1999. There may be several reasons for the apparent failure of leadership, which has impacted Nigeria's development negatively. Some of these reasons include: the underdevelopment of the education sector, which affects the quality of leaders and public servants generally; the culture of impunity which formed part of military rule, the remnants of which still plague democratic governance; the high costs of participation in the political process, which excludes the middle class and the intelligentsia from participation; the complex nature of the geopolitical dynamic in Nigeria; and the teething challenges that are faced by any nascent democracy.

The absence of good governance and effective leadership in Nigeria manifests in various ways, the most obvious being poverty, crime, insecurity, economic deprivation and increased income disparities. Nigerian citizens have responded to the consequences of leadership failings in various ways, some of which have resulted in changes to government policy or action. This paper seeks to examine citizens' responses to leadership failings as well as the corollaries of these responses to determine what kinds of citizen-led activism work best in the Nigerian context.

The paper commences with a brief review of the literature on leadership failings in Nigeria and the manifested consequences of these failings and then examines citizens' responses to leadership failings since 1999, and especially responses catalysed by technology and social media. The paper then concludes with an assessment on what kinds of citizen-led activism are most effective and how best citizens can tailor their responses to engender better governance.

Leadership failings in Nigeria

Leadership failings can take the form of dysfunctional leadership or the inability of leaders to meet up with the expectations of the followers or masses. Kelloway *et al.* (2004) summarized poor leadership as abusive, aggressive or punitive, and simply the absence of appropriate leadership skills. Eims (1996) views poor leadership as one that weakens the morale and motivation of citizens or the followers as the case may be. His study revealed that in situations where followers sense a failure of leadership or lack of responsibility by leaders, they would become resentful and in some cases choose not to be submissive to authority.

Eims's study is an apt reflection of the situation in Nigeria where many citizens are demotivated by poor political leadership, as evidenced by the lack of engagement of citizens in the political process. Ebegbulem (2012) argues that Nigerian society has never been well governed since independence from the British in 1960 because "good, strong leaders" have never been in charge. He highlighted that leadership failings can be seen in the lack of direction, neglect, insensitivity to the plight of the citizens, fraud and corruption that is characteristic of Nigeria.

A major evidence of leadership failing in Nigeria is the inability of the leaders to meet the expectations of the majority of followers. As stated by Neji (2011), it was widely expected that the return of Nigeria to democratic rule would bring about an improvement in development indicators. Following the return to democracy in 1999, after many years of military rule, citizens' expectation for good governance, efficient utilization of resources, transparency, account-ability and freedom of information were at an all-time high. The return to democracy was of course accompanied by ambitious promises from politicians seeking election into political offices. Consequently, many Nigerians expected an improvement in their living conditions and in Nigeria's development indica-tors and envisioned that Nigeria would become Africa's role model and a major global economic player.

Despite these expectations, little improvement has been made in Nigeria's development indicators. For instance, in the United Nations Development Programme (UNDP) Human Development Index (HDI), released in 2014, Nigeria ranked 152 out of 187 countries and featured among countries with the lowest HDI. In addition, Nigeria's Vision 2010, which was developed in 1997 and was aimed at positioning Nigeria to become a developed economy by 2010, now appears to have been a fantasy. One of the objectives of the plan was to ensure that by 2010, Nigeria would have attained 100% primary school enrolment rate and at least 26% of government budget (at federal, state and local levels) would be devoted to education. By 2010, Nigeria had the highest number of out-of-school children in the world at 10.5 million and education accounted for only 10.7% of the 2014 federal government budget, suggesting a failure of Nigerian leaders to achieve the set goals. This is in addition to inadequate housing and a limited infrastructure base, and the rising poverty levels in the country. According to the World Bank, 33.1% of Nigerians were living below the poverty line in 2014. There are however significant differences in the poverty rate by region, and while the south of Nigeria has a relatively low poverty rate at 16% in the south west and 28.8% in the south east, pov-erty rates in the north west and north east are 45.9% and 50.2%, respectively (World Bank, 2014).

Despite these developmental challenges, Nigeria's vast economic potential arising from its natural resource endowment and huge labour force, continue to raise citizens' expectations from the government for the implementation of policies that promote inclusive growth and improve living standards.

As discussed in the introduction, there are various causes for the leadership failings in Nigeria, which have been documented by several scholars. Some of these include Deng (1988) who is of the view that political power in Africa is "seen as an end in itself, rather than as a means for serving the people and producing tangible results in development and nation-building". Consequently, African leaders failed to develop institutions that would translate independence into popular democracy and liberty. This therefore led to the concentration of power in the hands of individuals, thus breeding inequality, abuse of human rights, injustice and repression of the citizens. In his study, Ochulor (2011) identified some factors as causes of leadership failings in Nigeria, such as: the lack of intellectual training and discipline of government officials; high demand for corruption and looting of public funds; limited participation of Nigerians in politics, which weakens the demand for accountability; pressures on public servants to take part in corrupt practices; emphasis on ethnic origin (tribalism); and weak emphasis on the rule of law.

The consequences of the leadership failings in Nigeria have been far-reaching. According to Agbor (2012), the result of poor leadership in Nigeria is manifested in consistent political crisis and insecurity, extreme poverty experienced by the majority of the population, debilitating corruption at all levels and rising unemployment indices. Ogundiya (2010) revealed that the consequences of leadership failure in Nigeria include: human rights abuses; political and bureaucratic corruption, which has resulted in increased poverty levels; insecurity; and a high crime rate. In his findings, Ebegbulem (2012) argued that abject poverty, inadequate health facilities and unemployment pervade the land and these are borne out of corruption and the failure of leadership. Ezukamma (2009) and Agbor (2012) both highlighted the high incidence of crime as a function of poverty, unemployment, underdevelopment and the criminality that the citizens witness on the part of the leaders. While the majority of the citizens languish in abject poverty and hunger, squalor, disease and destitution, Nigerian leaders enjoy a mind-boggling abundance, obtained through theft of state assets, cronyism and fraud. There is thus rising income inequality and a pervading sense of hopelessness among the populace.

Citizens' response to leadership failings

Citizens' response to government action is crucial in any country, as it evinces the extent to which citizens participate in government and police the leaders and hold them accountable by ensuring that their actions are in line with the demands of the citizenry. Citizens' responses play a significant role in the process of governance and the reaction of citizens to leadership failings influences the present and future conduct of office holders. Thus, appropriate citizens' feedback should affect the quality and nature of decisions made by the leadership and, on a larger scale, the quality of democracy in the country. Conversely, a lack of appropriate feedback can also mean that the quality of leadership does not significantly improve over time. According to Armstrong (2013), community and citizen participation is a critical element of strengthening local, national and regional communities and increasing the bonds and restoring trust between governments, service providers and citizens.

Since Nigeria attained independence from British rule in 1960, the country has experienced a series of citizens' movements in response to government actions and/or inactions. These movements have taken different forms to include riots, strikes, protests and demonstrations. In the 1970s, for instance, nationwide movements such as the Ali-Must-Go protest, rallied against the increase in the cost of student's meals by the military government. Also in the 1980s and 1990s, the Ekpan & Ogharefe Women's uprising, Anti-SAP (structural adjustment programme) riots and the 12 June 1993 riots were organized to either call for the practice of true democracy in the country or campaign for the formulation and implementation of favourable policies as well as the efficient management of the country's resources. Social and economic issues usually aggravated the different forms of civil disorder and disobedience, before and since the return to democratic rule in Nigeria in 1999.

Since the introduction of a democratic government in 1999, citizen efforts at influencing the actions of their leaders have increased and now also reflect the incorporation of digital platforms. The advent of the internet and mobile technology has resulted in the increased importance of social media to citizens' unrest and have engendered a structural change in the manner in which citizens react to issues of governance in different parts of the world.

The use of social media in response to government action led to online activism, which involves the use of social networking platforms such as Facebook, Twitter, Instagram and the use of mobile apps to raise awareness, share data and map social issues. Social media has triggered the participation of young individuals in matters of governance, politics, rule of law and citizens' rights and has been viewed as the modern platform for citizens with common beliefs to share their grievances and hold the government accountable, as experienced during the Arab Spring (Chokoshvili 2011).

Various studies have shown the importance of digital media to youth and their reliance on new media in contrast to traditional forms of media. According to Flanagin and Metzger (2008), digital media use and engagement data indicate that young people make up a decreasing share of traditional media consumers and rely more on new media to obtain their news and information.

The remainder of this section will examine different initiatives developed in response to governance failings in Nigeria between 1999 and 2014, while also illustrating government reaction to the demands of citizens.

The Nigerian Economic Summit Group

The Nigerian Economic Summit Group (NESG) was established during the military era in 1993 and formally incorporated as a not for profit organization in 1996. The NESG is a private sector-driven think-tank and advocacy group established to create a platform for improving the economy through dialogue and responsible private sector investment (NESG, 2015).

Although the NESG predates the time line for this study, it is mentioned here as it was the first coherent approach by the organized private sector in Nigeria to dialogue with, confront and challenge the military government over its failing economic policies, state-centric economic management and the mismanagement of the Nigerian economy. The NESG began by organizing a Nigerian Economic Summit in 1993, which was the catalyst for the first ever developmental aspiration plan for Nigeria: Vision 2010 (NESG, 2015). This plan has formed the basis for subsequent developmental plans and although the plan did not yield much fruit as was discussed earlier, it is notable as it was collaboratively developed by the public and private sectors.

The government's response to the establishment of the NESG was positive and since 1993, successive military and democratic governments have supported the Nigerian Economic Summit by attending at the highest levels, and by implementing Summit recommendations. In addition, since 2009, Nigerian ministers in council, through the Federal Executive Council, created a process to formally consider Summit recommendations and cascade to the relevant government departments.

Enough is Enough (EiE)

Enough is Enough Nigeria (EiE) is a non-partisan coalition of individuals and youth-led organizations committed to instituting a culture of good governance and public accountability in Nigeria through advocacy, activism and the mobilization of the youth population as responsible citizens (EiE, 2015).

The impetus towards the creation of Enough is Enough began during the period of late President Yaradua's illness in 2009. After returning from an extended medical trip to Saudi Arabia, the President did not appear in public for more than a month. This roused suspicions of a power vacuum, given the reports about his ill health. A group of individuals led by Chude Jideonwo organized a peaceful protest to the National Assembly on 16 March 2010. This was the first of several rallies that EiE would organize in response to government action on several critical issues at the time.

After the rallies, EiE decided to address citizen engagement through the electoral process as it considered that the more people are involved in the political process at various levels, the higher the likelihood that Nigerian citizens would be attentive to the actions of their leaders and hold them accountable. At present, EiE focuses on the youth demographic who are of voting age, i.e. those aged 18–35, who are engaged with technology through mobile phones, the internet and television. Using technology to spread information, EiE sends out a clear, simple message urging youths to Register, Select, Vote and Protect (R.S.V.P). In 2011, EiE also organized Nigeria's first youth-centric Presidential Debate in partnership with three other organizations.

In addition, EiE has created platforms to tackle issues that plague the election process in Nigeria. First is Revoda: a mobile phone application that turns citizens into election observers. Its unique feature is that it is tied to each user's polling unit (PU) number from their voter's registration card, which enhances geo-location, and allows EiE to send out messages to users that are specific to local governments, wards and polling units. The second version of this app allows citizens to report on other areas of public life. These are:

▶ **Electricity.** A simple interface that allows one to report when one has electricity. The data will be a powerful advocacy tool to counter official reports of electricity provided as well as allow factual dispute of the estimated bills that citizens currently pay

▶ **Corruption.** The app is linked to egunje.info or any other platform that tracks everyday acts of corruption by public officers such as police officers, court officials and civil servants. The goal is not to name and shame but to gather data that would be useful for advocacy and reform

▶ **NASS – ShineYourEye**, which is a platform to facilitate engagement with National Assembly members

▶ **Emergency/Crime.** Provide security tips, crime trends and database of numbers for security agencies

▶ **Polls and petitions**. An easy interface to respond to polls and sign petitions

Occupy Nigeria: January 2012 fuel subsidy protests

The fuel subsidy protests also known as "Occupy Nigeria" began on 2 January 2012 following the Federal Government's announcement of the deregulation of the Oil & Gas downstream sector on 1 January 2012. This announcement was accompanied by an immediate increase in the pump price of petrol to a prescribed average price of N140 from N65 per litre, representing an increase of 115%. The decision triggered a two week long industrial action and protests across Nigeria, causing a halt in commercial activities in many parts of the country and costing the economy an estimated N300 billion (US$2 billion).

The rationale for the government's increase in petrol price was the huge amount of public funds spent on subsidizing the domestic price of petroleum products (Moyo and Songwe, 2012). Under the subsidy scheme, the government issues import allocation licences to selected marketers, who are verified by the Petroleum Products Pricing Regulatory Agency (PPPRA), which subsequently repays the marketers the price differential over the government mandated domestic price of fuel. These payments accounted for up to 24% of the Federal Government's expenditure in 2011 (US$8 billion) leading to a debate over the sustainability of the scheme. In addition, the lack of efficient enforcement of the scheme became public as allegations of fraud were levelled against several marketers, the PPPRA and the Department of Petroleum Resources (DPR) (House of Representatives, 2012).

However, with the growing poverty and economic hardship in the country, many Nigerians viewed the government subsidy on petrol as the only real benefit derived from the government, the removal of which would result in more economic hardship and an increase in inflation. Given this background, Nigerians were aggravated by the increase in petrol price, resulting in mass protests, characterized by civil disobedience, demonstrations, strike action, and online activism calling for a corrupt-free government, a reduction in the cost of governance, efficient utilization of the country's revenue and the provision of basic amenities like power and infrastructure.

The severity of the strike action and protests led the government to partially reverse the subsidy removal policy and the pump price of petrol was reduced to N97 per litre on 16 January 2012, with the government continuing to subsidize a limited proportion of the fuel costs.

The protests also triggered investigations into the companies operating in the Oil & Gas downstream sector, which revealed irregularities and corruption among industry players. Investigations by the House of Representatives revealed that some marketers claimed subsidy on products not supplied, and 25 companies were indicted for fraudulent practises under the subsidy scheme (House of Representatives, 2012).

Another major outcome of the protest was the creation of the Subsidy Reinvestment and Empowerment Program (SURE-P), which was designed to ensure proper management of the saving that would accrue to the Federal Government from the partial withdrawal of subsidy. SURE-P is targeted at providing and improving social safety nets as well as infrastructure projects (SURE-P, 2015).

The Occupy Nigeria protest was a landmark event in Nigeria's history. Despite the vestigial memories of military suppression in Nigeria and routine government brutality towards protesters, Nigerians went against the establishment to demand a pivotal change in government policy. The reliance on social media in coordinating the protests did not stop with Occupy Nigeria, but went on to become an integral part of future movements. Although Occupy Nigeria was initially in response to the government removal of petrol subsidy, it has become a platform for Nigerians to express dissatisfaction with the management of the country's resources and in turn demand accountability and transparency in government.

BudgIT

In many jurisdictions, there is a move towards more transparency in government, through the sharing of government data on open data platforms. Organizations like the Open Government Partnership (OGP) have arisen to push for government openness, transparency and increased citizen participation in governance. Unfortunately, this is not yet the case in Nigeria and it is very difficult to obtain information on government actions, especially government spending. The lack of transparency applies to federal, state and local budgets and constrains demands for accountability.

This limited information on public spending and the resulting information asymmetry led to the emergence of an open data technology start up named BudgIT in 2011. BudgIT has a core goal of making the Nigerian budget simpler and accessible to the average citizen by converting budgetary statements into comprehensible infographics (BudgIT, 2015).

BudgIT also assists local communities to track public spending on community projects to ensure that these projects are completed (Onigbinde, 2015). By raising awareness, BudgIT increases the level of citizen demand for accountability as citizens equipped with information stand a better chance in their call for leadership accountability.

Despite BudgIT's success at raising citizen knowledge and participation in some communities, its small size and resources limit its level of impact. As a start-up, it can only tackle a limited number of states, and further, low literacy rates and low levels of internet penetration in rural areas, limit its efficacy. Reaching the critical mass of non- literate Nigerians will be essential to creating the pivotal level of accountability necessary.

Bring Back Our Girls

The #BringBackOurGirls movement is another example of how online advocacy can translate into offline citizen activity capable of gaining recognition on an international scale. The movement began due to tepid action from the Nigerian Government after the kidnap of 276 school girls from a secondary school board-ing house in the Chibok area of Borno State on 14 April 2014 by the terrorist group, Boko Haram (Bring Back Our Girls, 2015).

The kidnapping was followed by silence on the part of the Nigerian Govern-ment, and an immediate denial that it had occurred. In the aftermath of the kidnapping, the president's wife, Dame Patience Jonathan accused protesters from the Chibok community of attempting to embarrass the President (CNN, 2014). A sense of scepticism over the kidnap of these girls seemed to envelop the government, as many viewed it as a political detraction created to draw atten-tion from the World Economic Forum Africa (WEFA), due then to be hosted by Nigeria in May 2014.

On 4 May 2014, the President of Nigeria in a televised presidential media chat claimed that non-cooperation from the parents of the missing girls hampered government efforts to locate the missing girls. By then, the online campaign hash tagged #BringBackOurGirls had translated into organized action offline, led by the former government minister Dr Oby Ezekwesili and civil society leaders.

The protests garnered a lot of international attention, with prominent indi-viduals from all over the world taking up the cause. The international media consisting of CNN, Al Jazeera and others covered the rallies. During the WEF conference in Abuja, the issue of the kidnapped girls was frequently brought up, forcing the Nigerian President to address it during the conference. Also, the United States President, Barack Obama offered to send soldiers to support the Nigerian army in retrieving the girls (AA, 2014).

The international exposure successfully placed the usually secretive Nigerian military under scrutiny. The shortcomings of the military have become more obvious as the United States military became briefly involved in the search. The Pentagon's principal director for African Affairs accused the Nigerian military of pervasive corruption and theft of funding, which limited the Army's ability to curtail Boko Haram (Friend, 2014).

The effort to rescue the girls was ongoing in August 2015, and several other groups of abducted women and children were rescued between March and

June 2015. Although the Chibok girls have not yet been rescued, the campaign illustrates the power of the people to force government action on an issue and has managed to keep the situation of these girls in the spotlight. The immediate government response to the campaign was to establish a fact-finding committee on the abduction of the Chibok girls, charged with providing information on how the abduction took place. The committee submitted its report on 20 June 2014 and concluded that 276 girls were abducted, 57 escaped and 219 are still missing (Usman, 2014).

Although not necessarily a direct outcome of the Bring Back Our Girls campaign, the Safe Schools Initiative (SSI) was launched at the World Economic Forum 2014 (Africa) in response to the abduction and increased level of insecurity in educational institutions in northern Nigeria. Supported by the United Nations Special Envoy on Education and Nigerian business leaders, the SSI will invest an initial US$20 million aimed at creating safer learning environments in Nigeria (Gordon Brown, 2014).

Conclusion

As discussed above, leadership failings in Nigeria have been blamed for the low living standards and the failure to achieve key socio-economic goals such as the Vision 2010 and the Millennium Development Goals (MDGs).

However, citizen pressure in Nigeria is proving to be an effective mechanism to check the actions and/or inaction of the Nigerian Government and, in some cases, hold government accountable. Although the January 2012 fuel subsidy protests and the Bring Back Our Girls campaign may not have resulted in total adherence to citizens' demands, these events have and continue to show that citizens can set change in motion. They have also proven to be one of the effective methods of conveying citizens' concerns to the government, given their associated economic costs and government desire to prevent economic losses. The opportunities presented by social media if complemented by offline activism may be able to propel the desired change that is needed in Nigeria, and ensure that policymakers understand that citizens' interest should be a priority and at the centre of policymaking.

The discourse on leadership will improve when citizens understand that they have an active and obligatory role to play in governance, not only during elections, but in the conduct of leadership, and it is the responsibility of the people to hold their leaders to account. Although substantial changes may not occur overnight, an improvement in leadership may result when and if a critical mass of Nigerians comprehend the importance of citizen action.

As has been seen, the effects of citizen-led measures are mixed and many might not yield positive outcomes in the short to medium term. However, the rapid rate at which these movements arise demonstrates a positive trend in the development of Nigeria's democracy. The measures taken by citizens constitute the initial steps towards a more active and participatory democracy. By creating the foundation from which citizens can effectively critique, influence and drive discourse on the activities of the government, these citizen-led measures pave the way for bolder and stronger citizen engagement with the government.

In response, a more proactive governance style is beginning to develop. Some state governments are more open to critique and assessment of their activities. In February 2014, the Ekiti State Government invited social media activists to assess the infrastructural developments that had been made in the first tenure of the then governor. They were allowed to present any question or comment to the governor himself, however controversial. These questions were answered without reservation and a report of the assessment by these social media activists was then posted online.

Although citizen action in Nigeria cannot ultimately change the system from within, it can on occasion influence some of the decisions that the government takes. It is less certain if the effects of these citizen actions have any permanence to them. Permanent change might require citizen action from within the government; a goal that is notoriously difficult to attain due to the byzantine nature of the political system. Instituting critical change from within government has to be done from a level of high authority, and even then the scandal surrounding Nigeria's former Central Bank Governor, who alleged financial impropriety at the highest level in March 2014 and was suspended as a result, illustrates that opposition will still exist (Wallis 2014).

Finally, citizen engagement with the government in Nigeria must evolve from a constantly reactive one to a proactive approach—an approach that influences the decisions of government before they are made and one that spurs the government into making good decisions. That is the true essence of a democratic government: one where a synergy exists between the government and its citizens and citizen participation is a permanent feature of governance. In addition, citizen engagement in Nigeria has largely been a class-segmented affair made up of a middle-class majority. As a nation with a larger lower-class base, citizen-led engagement must extend to the majority of individuals. Citizen-led movements should aim to bolster the level of mass inclusion through advocacy, education and enlightenment of the populace on their rights as Nigerian citizens. Closing the language and literacy barrier will also improve the rate at which information reaches the masses and will significantly improve the effectiveness of citizen action in Nigeria.

References

Abiola, S. (2014). #Hope for Nigerians. Retrieved from http://www.project-syndicate.org.

Adeleke, F. (2011). Prospect and challenges of FOI Bill in Nigeria. Retrieved from http://www.elombah.com.

Adepoju, P. (2013). Q&A: SeunOnigbinde on BudgIT. Retrieved from http://www.humanipo.com.

Afolayan, A. (2012). A critical analysis of freedom of information act in Nigeria. Retrieved from www.odinakadotnet.wordpress.com/2012/08.

Agbor, U. (2012). Leadership behaviour and the crises of state failure in Nigeria: towards a transformational leadership attitude for addressing Nigeria's failing State. *Public Policy and Administration Research*, 2(4), 24-36.

Aminu, A., Kagu, B., Malgwi, Y., and Ibrahim, D. (2011). Analysis of Nigeria freedom of information act on records and office security management. *International Journal of e-Education, e-Business, e-Management and e-Learning*, 1(5), 396-400.

Applause Africa (AA) (2014). US army leads the search for the abducted 200 Chibok girls. Retrieved from http://www.applauseafrica.com/features/281-us-army-leads-the-search-for-the-abducted-200-chibok-girls.

Armstrong, E. (2013). The role of active participation and citizen engagement in good governance (UN Division of Public Administration and Development Management).

Bring Back Our Girls (2015). About us. Retrieved from http://www.bringbackourgirls.ng/about-us-2/what-is-bring-back-our-girls.

Brown, G., (2014). Statement by UN Special Envoy for Global Education, Gordon Brown. Nigeria joins safe schools initiative with $10 million commitment. Retrieved from http://educationenvoy.org/safeschoolsannouncement.

BudgIT (2015), About. Retrieved from http://www.yourbudgit.com/about.

Busari, S., (2010). Rare anger as Nigerian youths hit streets. Retrieved from http://edition.cnn.com.

Cann, O. (2014). Initiatives to promote skills and education launched at World Economic Forum on Africa. World Economic Forum. Retrieved from http://www.weforum.org/news/initiatives-promote-skills-and-education-launched-world-economic-forum-africa.

Central Bank of Nigeria (2012). Central Bank of Nigeria Communiqué No. 83 of the Monetary Policy Committee Meeting of Monday and Tuesday May 21 and 22, 2012.

ChannelsTV (2014). Jonathan Receives Report On Abducted Chibok Girls. Retrieved from http://www.channelstv.com/2014/06/20/jonathan-receives-report-on-abducted-chibok-girls.

Chokoshvili, D. (2011). The Role of the Internet in Democratic Transition: Case Study of the Arab Spring, Master's Thesis in Public Policy, Central European University.

CNN iReport, (2014). Patience Jonathan makes U turn, admits Chibok girls missing. Retrieved from http://ireport.cnn.com/docs/DOC-1133815.

Cole, E.A. (1997). *Personnel Management: Theory and Practice.* Fourth Edition. London: Letts Educational, Aldirie Place.

Deng, F.M. (1988). The Challenges of Leadership in African Development, Inaugural Programme of the African Leadership Forum. Retrieved from http://www.africaleadership.org/rc/the%20challenges%20of%20leadership%20in%20africa%20development.pdf.

Ebegbulem, C.J. (2012). Corruption and leadership crisis in Africa: Nigeria in focus. *International Journal of Business and Social Science*, 3(11), 221-227.

Eims, L. (1996). *Be a Motivational Leader: Lasting Leadership Principles.* Colorado: David C. Cook.

Enough is Enough Nigeria Coalition (2015). Why. Retrieved from http://eie.ng/about-us/eie-nigeria.

Ezukanma, T. (2009). Nigeria: Leadership and Crime, cited in Igwe, S., (2012) *How Africa Underdevelops Africa* (iUniverse, Bloomington Indiana), 4.

Federal Ministry of Finance (2013). Understanding the 2013 Budget.

Flanagin, A.J., and Metzger, M. (2008). Digital media and youth: Unparalleled opportunity and unprecedented responsibility. In M.J. Metzger, and A.J. Flanagin (Eds.), *Digital Media, Youth, and Credibility, The John D. and Catherine T. MacArthur Foundation Series on Digital Media and Learning* (pp. 5-28). Cambridge, MA: The MIT Press.

Friend, A. (2014). #Bring Back Our Girls: Addressing the Growing Threat of Boko Haram, Senate Committee on Foreign Relations Subcommittee on African Affairs.

Hassan, E. (2012, August 31). Occupy Nigeria: 'When the Cup is Full'. Retrieved from http://newpol.org.

House of Representatives. (2012). Report of the Ad-Hoc Committee to verify and determine the actual subsidy requirements and monitor the implementation of the subsidy regime in Nigeria. Resolution No HR.1/2012. Laid on 18th April 2012.

Imhonopi, D., and Ugochukwu, M. (2013). Leadership crisis and corruption in the Nigerian public sector: An albatross of national development. *The African Symposium: An Online Journal of the African Educational Research Network*, 13(1), 78-87.

Kelloway, E., Francis, N., and Barling, J. (2004). Poor leadership. Retrieved from http://faculty.london.edu/nsivanathan/PoorLeadership.pdf.

Kutsch, T. (2014). Anger swells against Nigeria government in response to girl abductions. Retrieved from http://america.aljazeera.com.

Lawal, T., Imokhuede, K., and Johnson, I. (2012). Governance crisis and the crisis of leadership in Nigeria. *International Journal of Academic Research in Business and Social Sciences*, 2(7), 185-191.

Milakovich, M. E. (2010). The Internet and increased citizen participation in government. Retrieved from http://www.jedem.org/article/view/22.

Moyo, N., and Songwe, V. (2012). Removal of fuel subsidies in Nigeria: An economic necessity and a political dilemma. Retrieved from http://www.brookings.edu/research/opinions/2012/01/10-fuel-subsidies-nigeria-songwe.

Neji, O.N. (2011). Civil society and democratic governance in Nigeria. *Journal of the Society of Peace Studies and Practice*, 111-125.

Newman, B., (1997). *Ten Laws of Leadership: Leading to success in a changing world*. Benin City: Marvelous Christian Publications.

Nigerian Economic Summit Group (2015). Our Mission and Vision. Retrieved from http://nesgroup.org/about.

Ochulor, C. (2011). Failure of leadership in Nigeria. *American Journal of Social and Management Sciences*, 2(3), 265-271.

Ogbeidi, M.M. (2012). Political leadership and corruption in Nigeria since 1960: A socio-economic analysis. *Journal of Nigerian Studies*, 1(2), 1-25.

Ogundiya, I. S., (2010). Democracy and good governance: Nigeria's dilemma. *African Journal of Political Science and International Relations*, 4(6), 201-208.

Okpi, A. (2014). FG spends N260bn on 30,000 ex-militants. *Punch Newspaper*. Retrieved from http://www.punchng.com/news/fg-spends-n260bn-on-30000-ex-militants.

Olua, C., (2012). Social media drives the #occupynigeria protest in Nigeria and across the world. Retrieved from http://is.gd/wq8vZx.

Omolayo, B. (2006). Leadership and Citizenship Development in Nigeria. In A. Agagu and F. Omotoso, (Eds) *Citizenship Education and Governmental Process*. General Studies Unit, University of Ado-Ekiti.

Onigbinde, S. (2015). Iwoye-Ilogbo Constituency Project: How BudgIT Intervened. Retrieved from http://www.yourbudgit.com/iwoye-ilogbo-constituency-project-how-budgit-intervened.

Platts (2014). Nigeria emerging as major importer of US jet fuel, kerosene: EIA. Retrieved from http://www.platts.com/latest-news/shipping/houston/nigeria-emerging-as-major-importer-of-us-jet-21551571.

Pointblanknews (2010). We reject 2010 budget: we demand 26% budgetary allocation to education. Retrieved from http://www.pointblanknews.com/pressrelease543.html

Techloy (2012). #OccupyNigeria movement gets website and Wikipedia page. Retrieved from http://is.gd/QDGVno.

Subsidy Reinvestment and Empowerment Program (SURE-P) (2015). History. Retrieved from http://sure-p.gov.ng/history.

The Nigerian Voice (2013, July 28). Child marriage: Senate will revisit the vote, says Mark. Retrieved from http://www.thenigerianvoice.com.

The Scoop (2013, July 25). #ChildNotBride: Mark says senate was blackmailed as Maina, Ezekwesili, Anenih, others pay visit. Retrieved from http://www.thescoopng.com.

Ukaegbu, C., (2010). Nigeria; Beyond Good Governance at 50. http://www.allafrica.com/stories/20100628063.html.

UNDP (2013). HDI values and rank changes in the 2013 Human Development Report: Nigeria. Human Development Report 2013. http://hdr.undp.org/sites/default/files/Country-Profiles/NGA.pdf.

United Nations Department of Economic and Social Affairs (2011). e-Government and New Technologies: Towards better citizen engagement for development - Report of the Expert Group Meeting. Retrieved from http://unpan1.un.org/intradoc/groups/public/documents/un/unpan047964.pdf.

Usman, T., (2014). Presidential Committee on Chibok girls submits report. *Premium Times*. Retrieved from http://www.premiumtimesng.com/news/163201-presidential-committee-chibok-schoolgirls-submits-report.html.

Vanguard (2013). 54% of Nigerian youths were unemployed in 2012. Retrieved from http://www.vanguardngr.com/2013/12/54-nigerian-youths-unemployed-2012.

Vanguard (2014). Ex-student unionist, Segun Okeowo of Ali must go fame dies at 73. Retrieved from http://www.vanguardngr.com/2014/01/ex-student-unionist-segun-okeowo-ali-must-go-fame-dies-73.

Vision 2010 Committee (1997) *Main Report*.

Wallis, W. (2014, February 20). Nigeria Suspends Central Bank Governor Lamido Sanusi. *Financial Times*.

World Bank (2013). Nigeria Economic Report. Retrieved from http://www-wds.worldbank.org/external/default/WDSContentServer/WDSP/IB/2013/05/14/000333037_20130514101211/Rendered/PDF/776840WP0Niger0Box0342041B00PUBLIC0.pdf.

World Bank (2014). Nigeria Economic Report. Retrieved from http://www-wds.worldbank.org/external/default/WDSContentServer/WDSP/IB/2014/07/23/000470435_20140723133415/Rendered/PDF/896300WP0Niger0Box0385289B00PUBLIC0.pdf.

DOI: [10.9774/GLEAF.4700.2015.de.00006]

Aiding and Abetting an Escape from Disciplinary Parochialism

A Case Study

Neil Stuart Eccles
University of South Africa

An ultimate task of responsible leaders is ensuring the just deployment of any command over natural forces that we are able to achieve. And it stands to reason that in order to achieve this, responsible leaders need, among other things, a well-developed sense of justice. An important precursor to developing such a sense of justice is the elimination, or more realistically, the reduction of bias. I argue that one source of bias which leaders might be burdened with stems from their disciplinary parochialism. In this paper I discuss a module taught to first year economic and management sciences students that specifically seeks the promotion of thinking beyond narrow confines of disciplinary canon. I describe how the module sets out to do this by constructing bridges using as materials the disciplines of moral and political philosophy and as tools the discipline of pedagogy. I then present reactions to the module from students, fellow faculty and selected external stakeholders. On the basis of these reactions, I cautiously conclude that the approach presented in this module might indeed be useful in aiding and abetting the escape from disciplinary parochialism.

- Responsible leadership
- Disciplinary parochialism
- Anti-solutionism
- Problem-posing pedagogy
- Infuriation

Neil Eccles is a professor and the Head of the Institute for Corporate Citizenship at the University of South Africa. He has a PhD in ecology and teaches moral and political philosophy to undergraduate economic and management sciences students. His primary research interests include responsible investment and teaching business ethics.

✉ Institute for Corporate Citizenship,
University of South Africa,
PO Box 392, Unisa, 0003,
South Africa

🖥 ecclens@unisa.ac.za

N HIS ESSAY ENTITLED "PHILOSOPHY for Laymen", Bertrand Russell (1950) reminds us that mankind is perpetually confronted with two problems. The first is the mastery of natural forces which, in the modern world at least, we typically tackle with scientific or technological solutions. The second is the *appropriate* deployment of any command over natural forces that we are able to achieve through our scientific prowess. It is the latter of these which is the realm of responsible leadership and Russell implores us not to lose sight of problems of this latter kind as we celebrate our achievements in terms of the former. He does this by vividly illustrating instances where our mastery of natural forces has been a source of human misery rather than wellbeing. Although some might contend that Russell's work is somewhat dated now, I would argue that the sentiment is no less relevant today than it was in the mid-20th century. And indeed some may even argue that it is more relevant (e.g. Morozov, 2013). In these technology obsessed times in which we now live, one might almost be forgiven for believing that building interdisciplinary bridges is simply a task of linking those who are seeking solutions to contemporary social ills with scientists who have the technological solutions but don't have the capacity to deploy them. In other words there is a risk that we become ensnared in the myth that the solutions to all social ills lie in the transfer of technical fixes from science to society across interdisciplinary bridges.

In this paper I make absolutely no attempt to engage in this type of interdisciplinary bridge building. Instead I focus squarely on the second of the two problems that Russell presents. In particular, rather than focusing on how we might build bridges between disciplines to trade technical solutions, I discuss an attempt to use different disciplines to construct bridges by which future economic and management science graduates[1] might escape from an imprisonment in narrow disciplinary parochialism. Why is the escape from disciplinary parochialism (or any other parochialism for that matter) important though? Well, the overarching rationale for this special issue is stated as making a contribution to "ensure a sustainable and equitable future" (Third International Conference on Responsible Leadership, 2014). This language implies nothing short of making a contribution to the pursuit of social justice, both intra- and inter-generationally. This recognition opens up a huge vista of philosophical thought, in which, arguably the most important contribution (as either a source of inspiration or target for critique) in the last hundred years was John Rawls's book, *A Theory of Justice* (1972). In this he elaborated at length on his simple and compelling idea of justice as fairness. In discussing this notion of justice as fairness, Sen (2010) has argued at length that a key precursor to realizing fairness is the removal of bias. And parochialism is a source of bias. To answer the question then of why bridges for escaping from disciplinary parochialism

---

1 Implicit in my reasoning here is the assumption that economic and management science graduates are disproportionately likely to take up leadership positions in society. This assumption is based on two things: First, on the increasing power wielded by the institution of business in society today; and second on the prevalence of economic and management science graduates as leaders within this institution.

are important in terms of responsible leadership in general and in this special issue in particular, my argument is as follows. Parochialism is bias; bias inevitably results in a breakdown of fairness; fairness is central to the achievement of justice; and the achievement of justice through responsible leadership is a driving rationale for this special issue.

Based on this line of reasoning, what I set out to do in this paper is quite simply to discuss a module that is taught to first year economic and management sciences students and that seeks the promotion of thinking beyond narrow confines of disciplinary canon. To use the language of this special issue, it sets out to do this by constructing bridges using as materials the disciplines of moral and political philosophy and as tools the discipline of pedagogy. I start out by describing the module with particular emphasis on the pedagogical tools used in its construction. Having done this, I then discuss some of the reactions to the module—both complimentary and critical—from a variety of corners including students, colleagues and one or two other external stakeholders.

"Sustainability and Greed"

This then brings me to a description of the module in question. The name of the module is "Sustainability and Greed". It is delivered to first year economic and management sciences students at the University of South Africa (Unisa), a large open distance learning university based in South Africa. Contemporary bureaucratic dictate in South Africa holds that modules taught in recognized universities must be described in certain ways. Among the key elements of such descriptions is the requirement that modules must have a defined purpose. The documented purpose of Sustainability and Greed is as follows:

> The overarching purposes of this signature module will be to remind commerce students of their humanity, and to present them with a primer to a lifetime of critical thinking. These objectives will be pursued by: a) introducing students to selected moral and political philosophy theories; and b) providing them with opportunities in the form of "case studies" to apply these to contemporary social themes associated with issues of sustainability and greed.

The module forms part of a university-wide programme known as the Signature Module programme. The idea behind this programme was that each college within the university would deliver a module to every student which would contribute directly to the aspiration that "every graduate leaving university is ready and equipped to make a difference—not only in the workplace, but in society at large" (from Unisawise, 2012, p. 15, cited in Louw, 2014). Whether one accepts the validity of this aspiration or not, the practical implication is that Sustainability and Greed is a compulsory module for all students hoping to receive an undergraduate qualification through the College of Economic and Management Sciences at the university. The module is delivered entirely online. All module content, student engagement and assignments are delivered via the university's Sakai-based learning management system known as myUnisa. Within this system, students are divided into groups of 50 and each group of students is assigned to a teaching assistant.

As mentioned in the introduction, the primary disciplinary materials used in the construction of the bridge are some introductory moral and political philosophy theories. These include both categorical and consequentialist (utilitarianism and egoism specifically) forms of moral reasoning. They include some aspects of distributive justice. And finally, they include some environmental ethics. Beyond this moral and political philosophy, the module also makes use of an interpretation of sustainability based on the relationship between the UNDP's Human Development Index and the Ecological Footprint similar to that presented in Eccles (2013).

Assessment in the module is achieved through a series of nine assignments. The first assignment is based on multiple choice questions. However, this is by no means conventional. The aim of this assignment is to force students to express an opinion on a set of issues relating to sustainability and greed before they have been exposed to any material or discussion. In a sense, students draw a line in the sand and then retain these views for future reflection. To do this, each question presents students with a statement and asks them to choose an option that most closely represents their view on the statement. Needless to say irrespective of which option they choose, they will get the associated grades since there are no right or wrong answers.

After completing this first assignment, students begin to cover the theory. At the end of each section, they are required to do another assignment. The majority of the next seven assignments involve interrogating one of the multiple choice questions posed in assignment 1 in more detail based on the particular body of theory presented. These seven subsequent assignments are submitted into public discussion forums and are thus visible to all of the students within the group as soon as they are submitted. Students are encouraged to engage with each other on their answers and teaching assistants are tasked with encouraging this debate by challenging student views, especially when these views appear to be tending towards "group-think". The ultimate aim is that students will construct a final submission for each of these assignments based on public engagement. The final assignment which students do in the semester has been labelled as a "summative portfolio" although it is really neither summative nor a portfolio. In fact is it simply a reflective final assignment. In this, students are required to redo the entire first assignment and to reflect on their final answers relative to their original answers with reference to the theory that they have learned and their engagement in the discussion forum assignments.

Pedagogical bridge building tools

While there is no real need to discuss in any depth the materials used in the construction of our bridges (the introductory moral and political philosophy), the pedagogical tools do require elaboration as they are somewhat unconventional.

Three basic ideas—theoretical suggestions if you like—"locate" the more inter-esting aspects of the module's pedagogical design from the perspective of aid-ing and abetting the escape from disciplinary parochialism. The first two are Evgeny Morozov's (2013) notion of solutionism and Paulo Freire's (1970) idea of a problem posing pedagogy. These are quite closely related and I will discuss them together. The third is Alasdair MacIntyre's (1967) description of Socrates' use of infuriation as an approach to the teaching of ethics.

Anti-solutionism and problem posing

Solutionism as defined by Morozov is a concern, reminiscent of Russell's con-cern discussed in the introduction, regarding an over-inflated expectation that technology will solve all of our problems. In Morozov's own words:

> Recasting all complex social situations either as neat problems with definite, com-putable solutions or as transparent and self-evident processes that can be easily optimized—if only the right algorithms are in place!—this quest is likely to have unexpected consequences that could eventually cause more damage than the prob-lems they seek to address. I call the ideology that legitimizes and sanctions such aspirations "solutionism" (Morozov, 2013, p. 5).

In his contemplation of the undesirability of this solutionism, Morozov envi-sions many types of "damage":

> Imperfection, ambiguity, opacity, disorder, and the opportunity to err, to sin, to do the wrong thing: all of these are constitutive of human freedom, and any concen-trated attempt to root them out will root out that freedom as well. If we don't find the strength and the courage to escape the silicon mentality that fuels much of the current quest for technological perfection, we risk finding ourselves with a politics devoid of everything that makes politics desirable, with humans who have lost their basic capacity for moral reasoning, with lackluster (if not moribund) cultural insti-tutions that don't take risks and only care about their financial bottom lines, and, most terrifyingly, with a perfectly controlled social environment that would make dissent not just impossible but possibly even unthinkable (Morozov, 2013, p. xiv).

Besides these types of damage, Morozov importantly also envisages a form of leadership myopia. We have all no doubt been confronted with the mantra "don't bring me problems, bring me solutions". Nine times out of ten this will emanate from a manager or leader to whom we report. The simple consequence of this is that, by their own instructions, problems that defy trivial solutions parochially specified in disciplinary canon are often not conveyed to leaders. Or as Morozov puts it: "What worries me most is that, nowadays, the very availability of cheap and diverse digital fixes tells us what needs fixing" (Morozov, 2013, p. xv).

It is this specific concern raised by Morozov, slightly generalized and in another sense slightly focused, which is important in terms of framing Sus-tainability and Greed. It is generalized in the sense that we do not restrict our concern to an obsession with "digital fixes", but rather an obsession with tech-nological fixes in general. It is focused since we contemplate solving the issue not in the general social sense, but in the very specific context of pedagogy and higher education practice in particular. Our broader social aspirations rely on a trickle down model.

We now turn our attention to Freire's (1970) idea of a problem posing pedagogy. Before interrogating the application of this, it is perhaps useful to understand Freire's ultimate goal in proposing this approach. Quite simply put, like many of us, Freire objected to oppression. Furthermore, Freire contended that the liberation of the oppressed (and indeed the liberation of the oppressors) can only emerge from the oppressed themselves. It cannot be imposed by the oppressors. In other words, liberation is the "task of the oppressed" (Freire, 1970, p. 26). This, however, presented some challenges. Not least among these were the challenges posed by Antonio Gramsci's idea of the cultural hegemony and the associated intellectual leadership exercised by oppressors (Fontana, 2002). Freire did not shy away from this challenge however. In fact, overcoming this and empowering the oppressed to take up their task of liberation was precisely the purpose of Freire's efforts. And central to this according to Freire was the following:

> In order for the oppressed to be able to wage the struggle for their liberation, they must perceive the reality of oppression not as a closed world from which there is no exit, but as a limiting situation which they can transform (Freire, 1970, p. 31).

This led Freire into a discussion on teaching. In this he started out with a critique of the prevailing paradigm of teaching which he described as the banking concept of education. Here he used the metaphor of the teacher simply making deposits of knowledge into the students which they in turn would be expected to memorize and reproduce with high fidelity. Freire contended that such an approach stifles creativity and incredulity among students and as such is very likely to simply support any entrenched hegemony. Or as Giroux (2011) puts it, it is an approach that is likely to simply reproduce what has always been. In doing this, it is a concept of education which really is ill equipped to allow people to "perceive the reality of oppression" particularly when that banking approach emphasizes deposits of known solutions—a solutionist banking approach if you like.

As an alternative, Freire presented his problem posing pedagogy. Here the first role of the teacher is very explicitly to allow students to "perceive the reality of oppression". According to Freire, this is achieved by posing the problems (or if you like the contradictions) of their existence to students. Once this task is completed, the student and teacher can engage as equals in co-imagining more just ways of doing things, and importantly pursuing these more just ways as practice—the notion of praxis. Freire's conception of problem posing pedagogy encompasses all of this: the posing of problems; the co-imagining of more just ways; and the struggle to see these just ways put into practice. In terms of this module, it is of course clear that we are not seeking a pedagogy for the oppressed per se. Although privilege is a rather broad term, it is reasonably safe to argue that undergraduate university students typically do not represent a subaltern class. And indeed, as already argued, it seems reasonable to suppose that a disproportionate number of these students are likely to progress to leadership positions, certainly in the institution of business. In spite of this fact that we were not seeking a pedagogy for the oppressed, it should be immediately clear how the problem posing pedagogy presents a great deal of promise as an antidote to solutionism, and in terms of facilitating an escape from the confines of parochial positions.

In terms of our actual application of problem posing as an antidote for solutionism and as a tool for constructing escape bridges, the module "Welcome message" clearly articulates our intent to students as follows: "This module is meant to confuse you. It's meant to force you to scratch your head. It's meant to force you to question things and to wonder. And it's meant to force you to think." To do this, the module poses an awful lot of very profound problems associated with intra- and inter-generational justice to students and really does not propose any solutions. Problems formally posed include (in no specific order) issues of child mortality, executive remuneration, overexploitation of natural resources (all illustrated in Box 1), climate change, economic inequality, the nature and purpose of business in society, human population growth, and global financial crises. One might imagine that in presenting the moral and political philosophy which we provide as the theoretical core, solutions might be prescribed. However, this is about as far from the reality of the module as it is possible to imagine. We spend almost as much time outlining problems associated with particular philosophies as we do describing their merits. In our assignments we specifically seek out examples where the application of philosophy leads to uncomfortable conclusions—infuriation points as I discuss in the next section. And wherever possible we juxtapose one philosophy against another to show that for these profoundly important problems there are really no simple algorithmic moral solutions. In short, contrary to the calls from authors such as Mathison (1988),[2] we make no attempt whatsoever to pull all the theories together into some sort of simple instrumental framework to spare economic and management sciences students the burden of actually having to think philosophically about social issues.

Through our discussion-based assignments, we do of course encourage our students to propose their own solutions. However, we encourage them even more strongly to engage with each other robustly around the usefulness or otherwise of these solutions. In this we take heed of Freire's (1970, p. 66) assertion that: "Any situation in which some individuals prevent others from engaging in the process of inquiry is one of violence." Finally, I remember as an undergraduate student "hanging out" with engineering students and having

---

2 Mathison (1988) argued among other things that business ethics courses presented to business students were "not speaking to real business persons facing real business problems" (p. 777). He argued that these courses had "an excessively philosophical bent more akin to the classics department" (p. 777). Furthermore, he argued somewhat paradoxically that philosophical thinking "is fine, even preferred, in advanced academic study but it may not cut it with business students especially if philosophy is applied to ethical decision making" (p. 779). Since ethics is technically a branch of philosophy, it is difficult to see how the separation can really be contemplated. As an alternative he presented a number of simplified algorithmic decision making protocols which could be delivered to business students to protect them from exposure to the philosophy.

them relate to me that their lecturers were at great pains to inform them that when they graduated, they were not to consider themselves qualified. True qualification would take years of practice. Likewise, our intention here is not to produce qualified students. Our intention is to start students on a journey of qualification. Indeed, in this case, if the job is done correctly this journey ought never to end. Once again, to borrow from Freire: "The unfinished character of human beings and the transformational character of reality necessitate that education be an ongoing activity" (Freire 1970, p. 65).

Infuriation

This then brings me to the third basic pedagogical tool used in the construction of our escape bridges. The essence of this idea is captured in the following quote from MacIntyre (1967) in his discussion of Socrates' approach to the teaching of ethics: "...infuriating someone may indeed be the only method of disturbing him sufficiently to force him into philosophical reflection on moral matters" (MacIntyre, 1967, p. 20).[3] This is the idea of infuriation as a pedagogical tool, a tool which seems to be at least as old as Western philosophy. In this approach, the aim is to disturb students out of their comfortable parochialism.

The most obvious infuriation point in the module is without a doubt the name of the module—"Sustainability and Greed". The word "Greed" was chosen with an awareness that in economic and management circles greed is a bit of a sensitive issue and with an appreciation that its use would likely evoke some discomfort. Following on from the name, the next barrage of potential infuriation points which students are confronted with are the multiple choice questions in assignment 1. Both the statements which are presented to students and the options from which students are asked to choose were carefully selected to provoke outrage from as broad an array of students as possible. Three examples are presented in Box 1.

---

3 A similar sentiment is expressed by Sen (2010) in his discussion of "Wrath and Reasoning" (p. 390).

Box 1 Examples of potentially infuriating multiple choice questions posed to students

6. "Every day some 20,000 children die prematurely from poverty related causes, mostly treatable diseases." My personal opinion on this statement is most closely described by:
   a) Who cares?
   b) It's hard to say it, but given the rising human population, perhaps this is a blessing in disguise for the human species as a whole.
   c) It's hard to say it, but this just means less people competing with me for scarce opportunities and resources.
   d) This is morally wrong, but practically, I think that it would cost too much money to solve.
   e) It is morally unacceptable for a single child to die of a preventable disease and we should collectively fix this irrespective of the cost.

10. "In 2010, Whitey Basson, the CEO of Shoprite, earned ZAR620,000,000.00." My personal opinion on this statement is most closely described by:
   a) Who cares?
   b) Good for him—he worked hard to earn this.
   c) The only problem I have with this is that this money is in Basson's bank account and not in mine.
   d) I think that it is morally wrong for anyone to earn that much money.
   e) I think that active steps should be taken to correct such immoral executive remuneration practices.

14. "Save the rhino!!" My personal opinion on this statement is most closely described by:
   a) Why?
   b) Let the people who want to use this resource pay to protect it.
   c) We have bigger problems than worrying about rhinos.
   d) We must save the rhinos for our children.
   e) We must save the rhinos because it is the right thing to do.

In question 6, students are confronted with child mortality statistics and the fact that much of this mortality is preventable. We anticipated that being confronted with this in and of itself would be disturbing to many students. However, the real infuriation points were built into the options from which students can choose. Callous options such as "a) Who cares?" were chosen to really enrage students. In the second example (question 10, Box 1), students are presented with a somewhat extreme instance of executive remuneration to consider. We anticipated that student opinions on this matter were likely to be highly divided. We assumed that for many economic and management sciences students such remuneration practices would be aspirational—the point of studying accountancy or business rather than herpetology if you like. We anticipated that for this sector of the student body, options questioning the morality of such practices (d and e) might cause some outrage. At the other end of the spectrum we anticipated that many students might be concerned about the matter of economic inequality. For these students we hoped that options such as "b) Good for him—he worked hard to earn this" might not sit very comfortably. The third example in Box 1 considers the statement "Save the rhino!!" It was anticipated that the issue of rhino poaching would strike a chord with many students, particularly those from South Africa where the issue of rhino poaching receives a great deal of media attention. Once again, however, it is in the options that the real infuriation points are to be found. For any students with a concern for the plight of the rhino, options such as "a) Why?" were clearly chosen to infuriate.

Following on from assignment 1, the presentation of the philosophy begins. From an infuriation perspective this is, by and large, relatively benign. Admittedly, as alluded to in the preceding section, we conclude the presentation of each section of philosophy with a discussion of the inherent weaknesses associated with that tradition. If we are to believe Mathison (1988), then this might be expected to infuriate those students who have imbibed the mantra "don't bring me problems, bring me solutions". And in the section on sustainability, the fact that we contemplate genocide as a possible solution to our sustainability challenges may well infuriate some.[4]

However, efforts to infuriate resume in earnest in the assignments which follow each of the sections of theory. As already described, many of these interrogate further one or more of the multiple choice questions contained in the first assignment and the three questions in Box 1 are all examples of this. So, for example, in assignment 2, the multiple choice question on executive remuneration (question 10, Box 1) is examined more closely following the presentation on Kant's categorical imperative. Specifically, students use the categorical imperative to examine the morality of executive remuneration and then discuss their analysis. Although alternative interpretations are possible, the most likely outcome of the analysis is that remuneration such as this is immoral. We anticipated that this was likely to further outrage those students who are registered for their economic and management sciences degrees precisely in the hope that someday they will be remunerated in this way. Beyond this infuriation on an individual level, in any group of 50 students we felt it highly likely that there would be students who represent the school of thought that such remuneration is aspirational and students who think it completely unjust. We therefore anticipated the emergence of organic infuriation from the engagements between students in the public discussion forum.

The multiple choice question dealing with 20,000 children dying daily (question 6, Box 1) was used as a starting point for discussion in two of the subsequent assignments. Out of these two, it is assignment 3 which follows the presentation of utilitarianism which is perhaps most worthy of note. In this assignment we start out by asking students to do a Google image search using the phrase "child poverty". The images which emerge out of such a search are highly emotive

---

4 Of course we do this not because we want to advance genocide as a realistic solution. We do this to illustrate the magnitude of the problem and this is explicitly stated so that there can be no confusion.

and are likely to deepen any sense of outrage which the statement itself evoked. Students then consider the choices from a utilitarian perspective. In doing this, the most obvious (although by no means only) utilitarian option is "b) It's hard to say it, but given the rising human population, perhaps this is a blessing in disguise for the human species as a whole". We anticipated that it was safe to believe that in a group of 50 students this rather uncomfortable conclusion would emerge, and that this, together with ensuing group discussion would be provocative to say the least.

Finally, an interrogation of the "Save the rhino!!" multiple choice question forms the basis for assignment 6, which follows the presentation of environmental ethics theory to students. We once again use provocative imagery in the assignment description to reinforce any outrage that students might feel towards the issue at hand. However, the main infuriation point in this assignment comes when we say the following: "...now we are going to have a real discussion about this. As a starting point for this discussion, my preferred answer is: a) Why?" In crafting this assignment, it was anticipated that this would appear exceptionally callous to any student who felt particularly strongly about the plight of the rhino even though in the context of an academic exercise it is not at all an unreasonable question.

Those then are examples of what we hoped would be major formal infuriation points in the module. No doubt there are other points which will press the buttons of certain students, but these illustrate our design principle.

Reactions to the module

Students

Student reactions to the module seem to vary both from student to student and in the same student over the duration of the course. Very early on in the module students are invited to introduce themselves within their groups. By the time they do this most have read little more than the basic description of the module which usually contains the purpose statement and the welcome message where we tell them that this is a "crazy module" and articulate our intention to confuse them. Although students are not asked to describe what they feel about the module or what they anticipate from the module in these introductions, many do express views. Broadly speaking three positions emerge in these early engagements. The first is anxiety. This is an almost inevitable reaction to uncertainty and for economic and management sciences students being confronted with a module which is described with phrases such as "moral and political philosophy", "critical thinking", "sustainability", "greed", "crazy module", or "meant to confuse you" is surely likely to provoke a sense of uncertainty. No doubt the fact that this module is one of the few entirely online modules offered by Unisa contributes further to this anxiety. An example of such an anxious reaction would be something like: "I think I should check whether I really need to this module, your intro is quiet scary" (sic). Frequently, however, this anxiety is mixed with the second reaction to the module—some measure of curiosity. For example: "I am also a bit scared about this 'crazy module', however I look forward to its challenges and learning new things". Third, for a certain number of students, the module represents love at first sight. Or at least that is what they tell us. For example: "Okay I can honestly say I'm going to LOVE this course... Just finished reading the mini-lectures. Like WOW!"

What are generally missing from these early introductions are expressions of outright irritation at having to do this module in the first place. This is of course not surprising really. Most students will assume that lecturing staff who will be grading their work will not want to be told by students that they think this module is a waste of time. They will assume that such statements will preju- dice them when it comes to grading. However, that this sentiment does in fact exist emerges strongly in the final assignment. It emerges in two ways. Many students will tell us that when they started the module they anticipated that it would be a waste of time, but as the module progressed, they actually began to appreciate the module more and more. For example:

> Honestly when I started doing this module I said to myself what a waste of time, I even began to think that I was in a wrong course, but as I carried on doing the assignments my eyes got bigger my brain became wider and wiser with knowledge that I never thought I would have come across.

This change of heart is always comforting on some level. In contrast, some students remain convinced that the module is a waste of time to the bitter end. For example one student wrote in conclusion to the final assignment that: "I honestly can't say that I learned anything at all in this module... This module was truly a waste of my time and money." Ironically, such brutally honest views are actually an indication of some level of success. Through the course of a semester with us, it appears that some students have found the confidence to express their honest opinions in assignments for grades. If nothing else this is an indication that we have convinced them that any views can be expressed and that if they are appropriately supported they will be fairly graded. To use Freire's language, they have been liberated from a form of oppression inherent in the typical teacher–student relationship. And it is quite refreshing that some students at least have realized the benefits of infuriation as a tool to provoke people—in this case the lecturing staff—to reflect deeply.

In terms of the anti-solutionist and problem posing character of the module, we seldom get direct feedback from students. However, every now and then we get a student who has, for want of a better way of putting it, simply got it. For example:

> ...So [I anticipated that] this module would simply reiterate what I already know.

> Little did I know that this would be the most challenging subject I have ever come across? I have never spent more time thinking on any subject matter in my life. I also know that I will never complete this module as it will be a nagging reminder that I don't have all the answers and I have to constantly look to humanity rather than black and white fact throughout my life and career.

Student reactions to our attempts at infuriation are quite varied. Quite interestingly (perhaps a little worryingly), of all of the infuriation points in the module, the one that seems to provoke the most outrage from the student perspective is the "Save the rhino!!" assignment described above. Certainly it seems to provoke more outrage than the 20,000 children assignments. In particular our statement that "As a starting point for this discussion, my preferred answer is: a) Why?" seems to infuriate many students. Many will respond that this is a rather unfortunate indication of their lecturer's pig ignorance. An example of this would be: "This is in my opinion the answer of someone who is not informed about the ecosystem and its functioning. This might probably be due to genuine ignorance or because of indifference".

This example is of course quite polite. Many students are infuriated to the point of committing grave "interpretive violence" (from Walker, 1993, p. 4, cited in Morton, 1999, p. 3) on John Rawls' concept of the veil of ignorance by stating that this is a clear indication that their lecturer is shrouded in a veil of ignorance. So we see evidence of infuriation, but does this result in contemplation? As it turns out, evidence that this infuriation provokes thinking emerges most strongly in the assignment that immediately follows the "Save the rhino!!!" assignment. In this students are asked to calculate their own ecological footprint, and based on the demography of these students it is almost impossible that they will have a sustainable footprint. Being confronted with the possibility of their own unsustainability seems to force many students to revisit their outbursts about their lecturer's ignorance with a little bit more humility.

In the final analysis then, we might conclude that we have students who are affected to the point of critical thinking by the module and students who are really not. A handful of those that are affected may be affected to the point of being able to express their outright irritation at having their time wasted. For the rest, to borrow from the words of one such student, they are taken "out of [their] blissful comfort zone". This clearly implies some liberation from parochial constraints. While this is obviously not a guarantee that these students will go on to have a more sophisticated sense of justice and therefore be more likely to become responsible leaders, one might argue that at least this is a step in the right direction. In terms of those who are not affected, I would venture to speculate that there are also two groups. There are those who will simply never be affected. No doubt many of these will go on to become CEOs of large listed companies.[5] For these students, this module will be like any other in which they participate for the credits it provides towards their qualifications and which they forget about within an hour of submitting the final assignment. And finally there will be those who, in a year or five or ten will recall some part of this module and will then become affected.

---

5 In case you were wondering, that is meant to be an infuriation point in this paper.

Colleagues

In terms of colleagues within the College of Economic and Management Sciences, the module has had one major infuriation point: the name and specifically the inclusion of the word "Greed" in the name. Of course, had this been an obscure optional module, no doubt no one would have been the least bit interested. However, the fact that the module is: 1) compulsory for all undergraduate students in the college; and 2) supposed in some to way represent the college, meant that it was everyone's business. The original running title for the module was "Greed and Sustainability". This was presented to the college's management committee comprising the Dean, the Deputy Deans, the Tuition Manager and the Directors of Schools. After a very heated debate, it was agreed that the name would be changed to "Sustainability and Greed". Besides the slight softening of the name by putting "Sustainability" first, those opposed were eventually turned around by the argument that the fact the name was provoking debate in the meeting meant that it was doing exactly what it was supposed to do—induce thinking.

Following on from this, the name was presented to the Executive Committee (the Management Committee and the Heads of Departments) and Tuition Committee of College, and again debate proceeded along much the same lines. Those opposed to the use of the word "Greed" presented three arguments:

▶ That a name should reflect what a module sets out to teach, and it was presumed that this module did not set out to teach greed per se

▶ That external stakeholders and particularly industry might object to the use of the word "Greed", a prediction that did indeed materialize

▶ That students might object to having the word "Greed" on their academic records or worse, that their employability might in some way be compromised by this (to date such an objection has never materialized)

The argumentative anchor of those in favour of retaining the name remained that the debate which the name was provoking was a clear indication that it was a good name. After almost a year of debate in these various committees, the matter was eventually subjected to a vote in the College Executive Committee and those in favour of retaining the name won by a relatively narrow margin.

Other stakeholders

As already mentioned, there was a concern among some college colleagues that the use of the word "Greed" in the name, and indeed the module content beyond this, might infuriate certain external stakeholders, particularly those in industry. And indeed this did in fact materialize to an extent with one very specific industry sector representative body objecting most strongly to the module on the basis of the module description documentation. It transpired that it was the inclusion of "Greed" in the module name that initially provoked outrage and scrutiny. For some reason, this scrutiny led representatives from the sector to the belief that the purpose of this module was to sow seeds of incredulity among economic and management sciences students towards free-market capitalism. Of course this concern was only very partially true. The purpose of the module is to sow seeds of incredulity among economic and management sciences students towards everything, free-market capitalism included. This fact was perhaps best illustrated during written exchanges when the external commentators posed the question: "[The module] seems not to pay attention to Heyek, Nozick, Hume, Dewey, Smith, Rand or other of the early British and French philosophers or even to Pragmatic Ethics." To which we were able to answer: "In terms of Heyek, Nozick, Dewey, Smith, Rand or others, some of these are covered (notably Smith and Rand) and others are not. Other notable exclusions would be Aristotle and Marx."

Eventually a formal presentation with a more detailed explanation of the module was given to the industry representatives in question. The net result of this was that, while these representatives would have undoubtedly preferred to have a more conventional and instrumental teaching of business ethics (à la Mathison, 1988), the content was not entirely intolerable. The use of the word "Greed" in the name however remained as a major bone of contention and this discomfort will no doubt persist given the result of the college vote to retain the name.

These industry commentators were not the only stakeholders who expressed the view that a more Mathison-like instrumental teaching of business ethics would be preferable. Two commentators from universities outside of South Africa echoed this suggestion. Both suggested that the module ought to present students with some sort of moral reasoning framework for contemplating "real" business dilemmas. This suggestion has been ignored. First, as is apparent from the purpose statement above, the aim is not to deliver an instrumental business ethics module to our students but rather to provoke thinking and to encourage an escape from disciplinary parochialism. Second, bowing to these suggestions would run counter to our anti-solutionist and problem posing design principles. It remains our firm view that there is plenty of space elsewhere in curricula for the presentation of known solutions to deal with known problems.

Conclusion

The use of "Conclusion" here is perhaps more the consequence of tradition or habit than a true reflection of what actually follows. I really don't make any promise that a formal concrete conclusion is to be drawn. What I have done in this paper is describe a module bearing the name "Sustainability and Greed" and discuss some of the reactions to the module thus far. The module makes use of the disciplines of moral and political philosophy as the materials, and of the discipline of pedagogy as a toolkit, to construct bridges aimed at allowing economic and management sciences students to escape the parochial confines of their disciplines. I have not spent much time formally describing the moral and political philosophy materials as these are really not in any way unconventional. I have, however, described in some depth the pedagogical tools deployed which are indeed unconventional. In particular I have described how the design of this module was inspired by a sense of anti-solutionism, by a spirit of confronting students with problems associated with their realities, and by a desire to infuriate students to the point of thoughtfulness.

In terms of responses to the module, I present reactions from students, colleagues and some external groups. My impression is that these reactions seem a little out of the ordinary as far as university modules would normally be concerned. I hope that in presenting these selected reactions you will be left with some sense of the often heated dialogues which have emerged in and around the module. In no small measure, I use the fact that these dialogues have emerged to infer that the module might well be provoking thoughtfulness and in particular thoughtfulness beyond parochial disciplinary confines or comfort zones. No doubt this argument might be contested. However, notwithstanding the idiom that empty vessels make the most noise, I am a firm believer in the fact that when people are engaged in dialogue something must be going on between their ears and the probability that they may come to see the world through different, less parochial, lenses is likely to be noticeably improved.

If we then:

▶ Accept Sen's (2010) argument that less parochialism is likely to be an essential precursor for the development of a strong sense of justice

▶ And if we take it as axiomatic that without a strong sense of justice, leaders will never be able to bear the title of responsible leaders

▶ And if we bear in mind that a disproportionate number of students doing this module are likely to become future leaders in society...

...then we might be permitted to cautiously suggest that the approach presented in this module might be useful. However, I really do emphasize the word "cautiously". I harbour no ambition that this module be held up as some sort of model of demonstrated "best practice". In fact I believe that the notion of "best practice" is lacking in humility and rather unambitious. What I therefore conclude with is that this module is perhaps useful and is certainly a curiosity worthy of discussion, or interesting as a source of further provocation.

References

Eccles, N. (2013). Sustainable investment, Dickens, Malthus and Marx. *Journal of Sustainable Finance & Investment*, 3(4): 287-302.

Freire, P. (1970). *Pedagogy of the Oppressed*. London: Penguin Books.

Fontana, B. (2002). Hegemony and rhetoric: Political education in Gramsci. In C. Borg, J.A. Buttigieg, and P. Mayo (Eds.), *Gramsci and Education* (pp. 25-40). Lanham: Rowman & Littlefield Publishers.

Giroux, H.A. (2011). *On Critical Pedagogy.* New York: The Continuum International Publishing Group.

Louw, W. (2014). Designing learning experiences to prepare lifelong learners for the complexities of the workplace. In M. Coetzee (Ed.), *Psycho-social Career Meta-capacities* (pp. 307-320). Dordrecht: Springer.

MacIntyre, A. (1967). *A Short History of Ethics.* London: Routledge Classics.

Mathison, D.L. (1988). Business ethics cases and decision models: A call for relevancy in the classroom. *Journal of Business Ethics,* 7: 777-782.

Morozov, E. (2013). *To Save Everything Click Here.* Philadelphia: Perseus Books.

Morton, A.D. (1999). On Gramsci. *Politics,* 19(1): 1-8.

Rawls, J. (1970). *A Theory of Justice.* Cambridge, Massachusetts: Harvard University Press.

Russell, B. (1950). *Unpopular Essays.* London: Routledge.

Sen, A. (2010). *The Idea of Justice.* London: Penguin.

Third International Conference on Responsible Leadership (2014). Call for Papers, Albert Luthuli Centre for Responsible Leadership, University of Pretoria.

DOI: [10.9774/GLEAF.4700.2015.de.00007]

The Valuation of Ecosystem Services in South African Environmental Impact Assessments

Review of Selected Mining Case Studies and Implications for Policy

Joël R.A. Houdet
African Centre for Technology Studies, Kenya

Claudious Chikozho
Wits University, South Africa

- Mining
- Biodiversity
- Ecosystem services
- Impact assessment
- Valuation

Though the South African Mining and Biodiversity Guidelines were designed as a practical, user-friendly manual for integrating biodiversity considerations into the planning processes and managing biodiversity during the operational phases of a mine, from exploration through to closure, they do not specify exactly how ecosystem services can be assessed, in both non-monetary and monetary terms. The guidelines also do not indicate how the results of such assessments can be used in a meaningful way from the perspective of the mining sector and relevant stakeholders. This has led some mining houses and environmental impact assessment practitioners to explore ecosystem services valuation on a voluntary basis, going beyond legal requirements. Through the analysis of several case studies, this paper provides a critical analysis of how valuation of ecosystem services can be used to better inform mining project appraisal and management in South Africa. After discussing the main potential approaches to the valuation of ecosystem services within the mining life-cycle, we focus our attention on emerging valuation practices within the scope of environmental impact assessments and highlight the benefits and limitations of non-monetary and monetary valuation. We conclude by proposing the development of standardized guidelines and associated databases for assessing the net social and environmental impacts of mining in both non-monetary and monetary terms. Specific recommendations and research needs are also highlighted, towards producing information systems which would meaningfully link biophysical and economic data and enhance the decision-making capacity and leadership of mining companies, regulators and their stakeholders.

Dr **Joël R.A. Houdet** holds Senior Research Fellowships at the African Centre for Technology Studies (ACTS, Nairobi, Kenya) and the Albert Luthuli Centre for Responsible Leadership (ALCRL, University of Pretoria, South Africa). Joël is an expert on corporate natural capital accounting, valuation and reporting and is involved in several high profile initiatives, including the drafting of the Natural Capital Protocol and several work streams of the Intergovernmental Platform on Biodiversity and Ecosystem Services (IPBES). Dr Houdet also works as an independent consultant at Integrated Sustainability Services. Joël holds a PhD in Management Sciences from AgroParisTech (France), a Master's in Practicing Accounting from Monash University (Australia) and Bachelor of Sciences from Rhodes University (South Africa).

✉ African Centre for Technology Studies, Gigiri Court No:49, Off United Nations Crescent, PO Box 45917 – 00100, Nairobi, Kenya

🖳 j.houdet@acts-net.org

Dr **Claudious Chikozho** is a social scientist with over 16 years of experience in applied research in Africa. Over the years, he has acquired knowledge, experience and keen interest in integrated water resources management; rural and urban development planning; programme planning, monitoring and evaluation; public service delivery; and sustainable development processes. He is currently working as a Research Director at the Gauteng City-Region Observatory, Wits University, South Africa. His previous assignments include working as the Programme Director for the EXXARO Chair in Business & Biodiversity Leadership at the University of Pretoria; Science Uptake Coordinator at the International Water Management Institute in Accra, Ghana; Senior Researcher at the Council for Scientific & Industrial Research in Pretoria, South Africa; and Research Fellow and Lecturer at the University of Zimbabwe. Over the years, he has carried out several research and consultancy assignments and in the process, published more than 20 peer-reviewed journal papers and book chapters. His current research areas of special interest include public and private sector leadership and service delivery, sustainable development and technology transfer processes.

✉ GCRO, Wits University, Private Bag 3, Wits 2050, Braamfontein, Johannesburg, South Africa

🖳 claudious.chikozho@gcro.ac.za

Introduction

Background to the study: the negative environmental legacy of the mining industry

For many decades, South Africa has been relying heavily on mining activities to generate wealth that translates into economic development, infrastructure and employment. In terms of environmental management and rehabilitation, mining companies have a history of only complying with the absolute minimum requirements (e.g. Van Zyl *et al.*, 2012) and also following a reactive approach to managing impacts on biodiversity (Houdet *et al.*, 2012). At the same time, it is well-known that mining generally has substantial impacts on the latter. It has unfortunately left South Africa with an enormous negative economic, social and environmental legacy (McCarthy, 2011; Ramontja *et al.*, 2010; Swart, 2003). Many mining companies have been using irresponsible mining methods with no regard for protecting ecosystems and have often shirked their responsibility towards environmental rehabilitation by leaving an area un-rehabilitated before they are liquidated or leave the country. This negative legacy also relates to the long-term residual effects on the social, health and environmental well-being of communities residing in the vicinity of these un-rehabilitated mining areas (Swart, 2003).

Brief introduction to the 2013 Mining and Biodiversity Guidelines

The 2013 South African Mining and Biodiversity Guidelines (DEA *et al.*, 2013) were developed to partly address the environmental challenges facing the mining industry, with a focus on the conservation and sustainable use of biodiversity and ecosystem services. The guidelines' primary users were intended to be environmental assessment practitioners and mining companies when preparing environmental impact assessments (EIA) and environmental management plans (EMP), as required by law for all prospecting and mining applications. They were developed as a tool which would facilitate the development of the country's mineral resources in a way that minimizes the impact of mining on biodiversity and ecosystem services.

To that end, the guidelines were designed as "a practical, user-friendly manual for integrating biodiversity considerations into the planning processes and managing biodiversity during the operational phases of a mine, from exploration through to closure" (DEA *et al.*, 2013). They are thus based on six complementary principles (DEA *et al.*, 2013): 1) applying the law; 2) using the best available biodiversity information; 3) engaging stakeholders thoroughly; 4) using best practice environmental impact assessment to identify, assess and evaluate impacts on biodiversity; 5) applying the mitigation hierarchy in planning any mining-related activities (from impact avoidance to offset measures) and developing robust environmental management programmes (EMP); and 6) ensuring effective implementation of the EMP, including adaptive management. They also specify that a "range of tools and guidelines exist to support the application of these six principles". In other words, the guidelines include specific considerations with respect to each principle for each stage of the mining life-cycle (i.e. reconnaissance, prospection, mining and closure), including their implications for mining companies and decision-makers. Yet, they do not go as far as providing specific guidelines about how to value ecosystem services and how to imbed values meaningfully in each mining life-cycle phase and the associated business policies and practices.

Why should business value ecosystem services?

There are many definitions and classifications of "ecosystem services" (e.g. Haines-Young and Potschin, 2013; Landers and Nahlik, 2013; Millennium Ecosystem Assessment, 2005; Nahlik *et al.*, 2012). "Ecosystem services have become an oft used construct with which to describe, in general and also in very specific terms, benefits provided by nature and valued by people" (Landers and Nahlik, 2013). In essence, ecosystem services provide the benefits that human beings (including businesses) derive from ecosystems. According to the Common International Classification of Ecosystem Services (CICES;[1] Haines-Young and Potschin, 2013), ecosystem services can be classified into three categories: 1) provisioning services which generate beneficial goods, such as food and water; 2) regulating services which generate tangible benefits derived from ecosystem processes, such as flood, erosion and disease control; and 3) cultural services which generate social benefits obtained from experiencing ecosystems, such as recreation and spiritual values.

Governments, companies and citizens are often not aware of the benefits they receive from ecosystem services. Mainstream gross domestic product calculations and corporate decision-making and accounting systems are silent regarding the full value of ecosystem services, thereby giving the impression that reliable flows from well-functioning ecosystems have no value at all (Houdet *et al.*, 2014a; TEEB, 2010). As Comello *et al.* (2014) point out, a continuing challenge is the inability of firms to comprehensively understand (and sometimes the unwillingness to acknowledge) the connection between their actions and subsequent ecological impacts, coupled with an inability to consider firm-caused ecosystem impacts within existing decision-making and operational routines.

Because a lack of knowledge can lead to wrong decisions and even conflicts or catastrophes, a good understanding of ecosystem services, their benefits and trade-offs in development pathways is a prerequisite for win–win–win situations—when feasible—for people, business and nature (TEEB, 2010). The valuation of ecosystem services generates information regarding the links between ecosystem services and the benefits economic agents derive from them and could potentially be used in various business decision-making processes and applications. Valuation is thus increasingly being developed as a vehicle to integrate ecological understanding and economic considerations to redress the

---

1 http://cices.eu/

traditional neglect of business dependencies and impacts on ecosystem services in both private and public policy, decision-making and operations (Waage, 2014; Natural Capital Coalition, 2014).

Yet, for ecosystem services values to be used effectively in various business applications or decision-making processes, such values need to be expressed/ framed or made available in the appropriate format which effectively enables their intended use (i.e. concept of fitness for purpose). In doing so, businesses will be able to readily use them for strategic planning and investment decisions, internal management purposes (environmental management, supply chain management, budgeting and budget control), financial, sustainability and integrated reporting and disclosure, lobbying for the development of new market opportunities or informing ESG (environmental, social, governance) risk assessment (Houdet et al., 2012). This would also apply to EIAs and EMPs in the context of mining. This begs the question of the main approaches available for valuing ecosystems in mining.

Biodiversity and ecosystem valuation within the context of the SA Mining and Biodiversity Guidelines

Both qualitative and quantitative, non-monetary and monetary valuation methods can be used to value ecosystem services and the resulting values applied at various stages of project planning and management, e.g. in problem framing, project design, risk analysis and investment decision-making. On the one hand, non-monetary valuation methods include quantitative and qualitative research techniques (i.e. surveys, interviews), and participatory and deliberative tools (focus groups, citizens juries, participatory or rapid rural appraisal), as well as methods of expressing preferences in non-monetary but quantifiable terms (i.e. preference assessment, time use studies, Q-methodology) (Christie et al., 2012; Kelemen et al., 2014). Some studies also consider the spatial representation of ecosystem services through demand mapping and analytic tools rooted in biophysical approaches.

On the other hand, monetary valuation approaches include different methods which aim to put a monetary value on the use and non-use values of biodiversity and ecosystem services, the final choice of method depending notably on the type and availability of data. The judicious application of economic valuation techniques to ecosystem services can provide valuable information for conceptualizing decision choices and evaluating management options (TEEB, 2010), though some limitations in the economic welfare approach to decision-making have been extensively discussed by academics (e.g. Farrell, 2007).

It is also important to note that there are two main approaches to monetary valuation. As argued by Levrel et al. (2012), the first one focuses on opportunity cost assessment; i.e. typical cost–benefit analysis, which is based on weak sustainability[2] principles. The second approach involves cost-effectiveness assess-

---

2 **Weak sustainability** is the idea, within environmental economics, which states that natural capital can be substituted by financial capital.

ment of natural capital maintenance or restoration costs, which is grounded on strong sustainability[3] principles. While the opportunity cost approach can be useful to identify the most important types of benefits and costs of various ecosystem services to society, the maintenance or restoration cost approach aims to assess the minimal costs of achieving sustainable use and/or impact mitigation targets. Yet, which valuation approach is the most appropriate for mining companies to ensure the conservation and sustainable use of biodiversity and ecosystem services?

Aims and methodology

Because the guidelines only seek to provide pointers to existing biodiversity information and tools and how they can be used to integrate biodiversity considerations at every stage of the mining life-cycle (Shene-Verdoorn and Ncube, 2014), they do not go as far as providing specific guidelines about how to value ecosystem services, especially in monetary terms, and how to imbed the results meaningfully in each mining life-cycle phase. Mining companies and their EIA practitioners are thus left to decide which valuation approach to use.

This paper aims to critically analyze how valuation of ecosystem services can be used to better inform mining project appraisal and management in South Africa. After briefly describing the main potential approaches to the valuation of ecosystem services within the mining life-cycle, we focus our attention on emerging valuation practices within the scope of EIA. This is because this is the step which conditions how mining companies take into account ecosystem services throughout the life-cycle of their projects.

First, we explain the pros and cons of the main options for integrating the valuation of ecosystem services in EIA. Then, through the analysis of selected case studies, we discuss the benefits and limitations of non-monetary and monetary valuation. This allows us to highlight the need to develop standardized guidelines for assessing the net social and environmental impacts of mining in both non-monetary and monetary terms.

---

3 In contrast to weak sustainability, **strong sustainability** assumes that financial capital and natural capital are complementary, but not interchangeable.

Analysing emerging practices in the valuation of ecosystem services

Approaches to the valuation of ecosystem services in the mining life-cycle

The selection of an appropriate valuation method for a specific ecosystem services impact or dependency within any private or public decision-making process or activity requires making use of the fitness-for-purpose test: does (or can) the method(s) selected provide meaningful information to its targeted audience(s) for the intended purposes? It is therefore essential to emphasize that both non-monetary and monetary values are useful for decision-making and management purposes in the mining industry.

Table I presents a schematic view of the mining life-cycle from the perspective of the impact mitigation hierarchy, highlighting the corresponding valuation approaches and key questions which should be asked by mining companies and their stakeholders. For instance, biophysical values about the supply and use of ecosystem services (e.g. water producing areas, wetlands, threatened habitat) is critical to ensure that a proposed mine avoids the most important areas. Such information is also critical to ensure that impact minimization and rehabilitation measures are ecologically effective. With respect to monetary values of ecosystem services, while the opportunity cost approach is particularly relevant during the reconnaissance and prospective phases to identify important ecosystem services and their associated values for stakeholders, the maintenance/ restoration cost is without doubt the most pertinent approach from the perspective of a mining company's compliance with laws and regulations at the lowest possible cost.

Moreover, ecosystem services valuation, whether non-monetary or monetary, can be useful for:

▶ The environmental and social impact assessment so as to:

- Identify priority ecosystem services (e.g. no-go areas) and their associated values and benefits for affected stakeholders

- Make sure residual impacts are minimized as much as possible, for instance avoiding areas with ecosystem services values which cannot be offset

- Plan for impact avoidance, minimization, rehabilitation and offset measures (as part of the eventual Record of Decision were the project to be approved under specific conditions)

▶ The development of the environmental management plan which effectively deals with impact minimization and rehabilitation measures so as to minimize ecosystem services loss, as well as (potentially) plan for effective offset measures for those values which can be offset

▶ The development and updating of the closure and life-after-mining plan which can ensure that rehabilitated areas supply relevant ecosystem services to the relevant stakeholders, especially the surrounding communities

Table 1 Mining life-cycle from the perspective of the impact mitigation hierarchy, with associated main valuation approaches and key questions

	Reconnaissance	Prospecting	Mining	Closure	Life-after-mining
Application of the Impact Mitigation Hierarchy	Avoidance measures		Minimisation, rehabilitation and offset measures	Rehabilitation and offset measures	Offset measures
What is the main biophysical valuation approach for the mining company?	Biodiversity and ecosystem services risk assessment and mapping		Ecosystem services management mapping with associated impact mitigation measures		Identifying & securing ecosystem services equivalent to those which were lost due to mining
What is the main monetary valuation approach for the mining company?	Opportunity cost approach: Cost-benefit analysis of different mining options with different residual impacts		Cost-effectiveness approach: Comparative analysis of legal compliance options to minimise impact mitigation costs and liabilities (i.e. most cost-effective way to implement mitigation measures specified in Record of Decision and Water Use Licence)		
Key questions for the valuation of ecosystem services by the mining company	What are the ecosystem services in the receiving area(s)? Any critical one(s) used by stakeholders? What are the likely loss of ecosystem services and the associated costs to affected stakeholders due to the proposed mining project?		How can the loss of biodiversity and ecosystem services be minimised? Can ecosystems supplying ecosystem services be rehabilitated? Can biodiversity and ecosystem services loss be offset? If so, to what extent? What are the costs and benefits of implementing the mitigation hierarchy for biodiversity and ecosystem services? What are the most cost-effective options to reach the targeted levels of ecosystem services, ideally towards no-net-loss or net positive impacts (if feasible)?	Which ecosystem services can the rehabilitated areas offer to stakeholders? What are the associated costs and benefits to the mining company and its stakeholders? Is there a net loss of ecosystem services after closure? How effective was the implementation of the mitigation hierarchy?	

The valuation of ecosystem services in South African EIA: emerging practices and barriers to mainstreaming

There are, potentially, several options for integrating ecosystem services valuation in EIA for mining projects:

▶ The undertaking of specific, stand-alone assessments, making use of specific valuation approaches (non-monetary and/or monetary) as the mining house and/or valuation consultant see fit

▶ The integration of ecosystem services valuation, in non-monetary and/or monetary terms, in all relevant specialist studies, such as hydrology/water balance assessments, fauna and flora assessments, or social impacts assessments, making use of relevant valuation skills or expertise

▶ The integration of ecosystem services in a comprehensive and integrated specialist socio-economic impact assessment which would aim to assess the net impact of the proposed project, ideally in both non-monetary and monetary terms

While the first two options have already emerged to some extent in South Africa, as attested by our discussions with EIA practitioners and other field experts as well as desktop research (see case studies hereafter), we have found no attempt at undertaking option three within the scope of EIA. Indeed, specific, stand-alone ecosystem services specialist studies are increasing in number while some specialist studies (i.e. wetland, fauna and flora assessments at this stage) have started to integrate ecosystem services value assessments as part of their scope.

Table 2 presents an analysis of the pros and cons of each approach in terms of importance/visibility and usefulness for decision-making, data requirements, skills/capacity needs and costs, as well as timing/planning aspects. In essence, though stand-alone ecosystem services specialist studies may make the most sense in the short term, the second option could be actively pursued so that all specialist studies embed ecosystem services valuation as one of their outputs and hence produce values based on stronger biophysical data sets than stand-alone reports. On the other hand, undertaking comprehensive and integrated specialist socio-economic impact assessments presents a number of challenges to be discussed in more detail below.

Table 2 Pros and cons of the identified options for integrating ecosystem services valuation into EIAs

	OPTIONS FOR INTEGRATING ECOSYSTEM SERVICES VALUATION IN MINING EIA					
	Specific stand-alone assessments		Integration in all relevant specialist studies		Comprehensive & integrated specialist economic impact assessment	
	Pros	Cons	Pros	Cons	Pros	Cons
Importance/ visibility and usefulness for decision-making	Ecosystem services valuation is perceived as an important issue, worth an independent assessment	Difficulties in making meaningful inter-linkages between different specialists studies	Ecosystem services valuation is seen as an important component of all specialist studies, whether on hydrology, fauna and flora or social impacts	Ecosystem services values may be not visible if specialist studies do not bring them to the forefront	Imbeds ecosystem services values in the assessment of the economic impacts, both positive and negative, of the proposed mining project; Allows for the assessment of the net social, environmental and economic impact of the mine by putting a monetary value on ecosystem services dependencies and impacts, as well as associated internal and external costs and benefits.	Losses of ecosystem services, in monetary values, may not be commensurate to typical economic benefits of mining projects, depending on the valuation method used (i.e. maintenance / restoration cost approach may tend to generate higher values based on a target of a no-net-loss than opportunity cost approaches); Monetary values cannot be the sole basis for decision-making.

Continued

	OPTIONS FOR INTEGRATING ECOSYSTEM SERVICES VALUATION IN MINING EIA					
	Specific stand-alone assessments		Integration in all relevant specialist studies		Comprehensive & integrated specialist economic impact assessment	
	Pros	Cons	Pros	Cons	Pros	Cons
Data requirements	Some simple valuation methods are accessible (e.g. ecosystem services mapping and ranking)	Biophysical data to be used for valuation may be lacking, due to the lack of alignment / cooperation with other specialists or the lack of appropriate database; Relevant economic data (e.g. only value transfer methods possible due to budget constraints) may also be lacking and affect the quality of the study.	ToRs of specialist studies may be tailored to produce biophysical data relevant to ecosystem services valuation. Some simple non-monetary valuation methods are accessible (e.g. ecosystem services mapping and ranking).	Relevant economic data may be lacking and affect the quality of the study (e.g. only value transfer methods possible due to budget constraints).	—	Biophysical data required for economic valuation may be lacking. Lack of alignment with specialist studies may be an issue. Unreliable value transfer methods may be used due to lack of budget. Social Accounting Matrices typically used do not account for externalities, which would force specialists to develop new / complementary models (more expensive).

Skills / capacity needs	All required specialists (environmental / biophysical and economic expertise) are available in the market; Niche market development and entrepreneurship may be encouraged.	Biophysical specialists (e.g. wetlands, hydrology, fauna & flora) and economists need to work together; Work quality standards may be an issue; Mining houses and EIPs need to be aware of this for the drafting of ToRs and the selection of consultants.	All specialists would get a better understanding of the values of ecosystem services linked to their biophysical assessments	Would require additional capacity building / training for all specialists, the recruitment of economists by EIPs and / or a mix of both	Would promote integrated thinking and skills development by making economists and natural scientists work together	Would take time and commitments to get people from different disciplines working together in an effective way
Costs	Simple monetary valuation methods (value transfer) are available in certain contexts (i.e. relevant comparable data available) to minimise costs	Mining houses and EIPs need to cater for additional costs, which can be significant in certain circumstances	This may be part of continuing professional development to some extent	Additional training costs and / or hiring may be expensive	May save costs to society by provided a more complete picture of net benefits of the proposed mining project	Significantly increases in the scope and workload for consultants when compared to that of standard economic impact assessments; Additional budgets would have to be secured by project developers.

Continued

OPTIONS FOR INTEGRATING ECOSYSTEM SERVICES VALUATION IN MINING EIA

	Specific stand-alone assessments		Integration in all relevant specialist studies		Comprehensive & integrated specialist economic impact assessment	
	Pros	Cons	Pros	Cons	Pros	Cons
Timing / planning	Can be undertaken at the same time as other specialist studies if all relevant data is available	May require data which can only be supplied by other specialist studies and, hence, result in delays	Undertaken within the timeframe of specialist study concerned	–	Can be undertaken at the same time as other specialist studies if all relevant data is available	May require data which can only be supplied by other specialist studies and, hence, result in delays
Likelihood to be used by EIPs and mining houses	Studies already available in the market, but essentially making use of quantitative non-monetary valuation methods; No requirement to undertake them by law limits uptake; IFC Performance Standards 6 is the key driver, used mainly for mining projects with international financing arrangements.		Some fauna and flora studies incorporate ecosystem services assessment components, for instance for that of wetlands; No requirement to undertake them by law limits uptake; IFC Performance Standards 6 is the key driver, used mainly for mining projects with international financing arrangements.		No study in South Africa identified by the authors; The additional skills, data requirements and costs involve significant transaction costs not likely to be willingly accepted by mining companies; All stakeholders would need to cooperate to fund the development of the supporting data infrastructure.	

The benefits and limitations of non-monetary ecosystem services assessments

Typical ecosystem services assessments currently carried out for EIA of mining projects in South Africa involve the quantitative non-monetary scoring of different ecosystem services. For instance, the draft EIA-EMP for the proposed Zonnebloem Coal Mine in Mpumalanga, South Africa, included the results of a functional assessment of the wetlands (Wetland Consulting Services, 2013) using the Wet-EcoServices methodology (Kotze et al., 2009). This method provides a scoring system for establishing wetland ecosystem services. With scores varying from 0 (not able to perform the function) to 4 (fully functional), it enables one to make relative comparisons of systems based on a logical framework that measures the likelihood that a wetland is able to perform certain functions.

The Wet-EcoServices methodology produced a clear visual understanding of the main ecosystem functions of the wetlands to be impacted by the proposed coal mine. It further allowed consultants to make pragmatic recommendations for wetland impact avoidance, minimization and offset measures as part of the EMP; notably by helping define and quantify wetland offset requirements. In other words, this habitat-specific tool can provide meaningful information about the potential functions and services from wetlands and hence help improve decision-making regarding the implementation of the impact mitigation hierarchy.

Another example is that of the "ECO-FUTURES" Ecosystem Services Supply and Demand Assessment (FutureWorks, 2013), which was used for the same proposed coal mine, mainly to: 1) identify the ecosystem services which currently benefit local communities and downstream users, as well as provincial and national users; 2) assess the dependence of beneficiaries or users on the supply of these ecosystem services; and 3) assess, based on comparison of supply and demand, the risk to priority ecosystem services with the development of the Zonnebloem Coal Mine.

This was done by scoring the condition of the land cover types, identifying the priority ecosystem services supplied, scoring the capability of the land cover types to supply these services under pristine conditions and developing a number of future scenarios.

This is a relatively comprehensive exercise as it involves all land-use types, though at a higher, less accurate level than the Wet-EcoServices methodology that is only applicable to wetlands. Scoring by experts and key stakeholders, typically through focus groups, does constitute an interesting and useful way to express the value(s) of ecosystem services to different stakeholders and the associated risks due to land-use changes, under different scenarios, and this while avoiding undertaking time-consuming and expensive quantitative biophysical data collection.

Yet, both examples and associated methods also have limitations. They provide multi-criteria results which may lead to conflicting results (e.g. it is difficult to compare scenarios) and fall short of providing relevant information for use in the economic impact assessment of the proposed mining project: e.g. economic data regarding the current availability/supply of ecosystem services and the potential losses of the latter for various stakeholder groups due to the proposed mine. Indeed, economic information would constitute critical information for making an informed decision about the economic net benefits of the proposed mine from the perspective of decision-makers and relevant government departments pushing for economic development. But there are rare examples in South Africa where efforts have been made to quantify in monetary terms the loss of ecosystem services within the scope of an EIA. The following section proposes a critical analysis of a case study.

A critical study of a cost–benefit analysis involving monetary ecosystem services values

An economic impact assessment[4] for a coal mining project (NBC: Belfast Project) in Mpumalanga, South Africa was undertaken and included an "Ecosystem Services Analysis" for 378 ha of wetlands found within the proposed mining area which falls into the Nkomati catchment (Golder Associates, 2009). Though the authors explained that the analysis did not fall within the brief given by the client, they wanted to show the potential value of wetland benefits enjoyed by broader society because of potential future liability implications for the mining company degrading the wetlands, as well as changes in public and shareholder perceptions of corporate social responsibility.

To that end, the authors used an opportunity cost approach and, more specifically, benefit transfer techniques to assess the values of ecosystem services from the area (i.e. using values per ha from other studies). This is clearly the least expensive approach available. The affected wetlands were thus estimated to potentially supply ecosystem services to the value of between ZAR3 million and ZAR120 million per year to onsite as well as downstream users (Golder Associates, 2009). Yet, did the results satisfy the study aims?

On the one hand, the study does give an indication of potential economic benefits of the affected wetlands to the broader society. On the other hand, it fails to provide an idea of potential future liability implications due to wetland loss or degradation as no explanation is given to provide a clear link between specific ecosystem services values, any legal obligations or regulations and/or the potential loss of economic activity or livelihood onsite or for downstream users which may lead to litigation (and hence potential liabilities). Taking into account potential legal biodiversity or water offset requirements would have led the authors to tell another story. How much could the replacement of lost wetlands potentially cost the project developer? How much land would need to be purchased, managed and/or rehabilitated to reach no net loss of biodiversity or wetland functionality (i.e. water purification capacity)? Answering those questions would require using different economic valuation tools, namely replacement and restoration cost methods, and would be more time consuming. This point clearly questions the adequacy of the valuation model design.

---

4 The assessment was called a "Sustainable Development Investigation".

Furthermore, there is a very limited assessment of the social consequences of the loss of the wetland ecosystem services, as no livelihood or social/business activity depending on wetland ecosystem services specific to the study site is discussed. Only potential ecosystem services benefits according to other studies based on other wetlands are used. Accordingly, it is difficult to assess whether the project will have any tangible impact on specific stakeholder groups, and the authors logically call for further in-depth studies. Besides, no assessment of the cost implications of impact avoidance and mitigation and proposed social spending to support communities or stakeholders who would be affected is discussed. These would have provided valuable information for decision-making about whether or not to approve the mining project.

What is more, the monetary values of wetland services were not integrated in the broader cost–benefit analysis undertaken. If one does so, we would compare the loss of wetland benefits with the economic impacts of the main mining scenario. The latter has a potential total production impact of R121.5 billion and a potential total regional GDP contribution of R41.6 billion over a 100 year horizon (Golder Associates, 2009). In that context, R0.123 billion/year of lost wetland services over 100 years may seem a lot or relatively little (total of R12.3 billion, or just a bit more than 10% of the total production impact), depending on the stakeholder perspective. But is this loss acceptable? The study unfortunately did not attempt to explain whether this was the case.

One can therefore argue that the information provided and subsequent analysis undertaken were insufficient to support fully informed decision-making. This calls into question the need for greater clarity on the type of economic impact assessment required to assess the positive and negative social and environmental externalities of proposed mining projects.

Assessing the net social and environmental impacts of mining projects in economic terms

The limits of typical cost–benefit analysis of mining projects

Economic impact assessments in mining typically deal with the evaluation of potential impacts, both positive and negative, of a particular project on the economy of the receiving area, at the local, regional and/or national level. These cost–benefit analyzes assess the potential changes in production output, gross value added and employment during all relevant life-cycle phases of the proposed mining project (i.e. construction, operations, closure, land-use after mining). This requires knowledge of expenditure on the construction of the mine and operating costs borne once mining commences. Conversion of these input data into economic impacts is done by using an econometric model.

Typically, national social accounting matrices and associated multipliers are used as the primary database for such cost–benefit analyzes. These are comprehensive, economy-wide databases that contain information about the flow of economic resources between the different economic agents in an economy. These models therefore have the ability to quantify the impact of economic events on the various sectors and agents in the economy and also show the aggregated effect on the macro-economic variables on the total economy.

Yet, national social accounting matrices and associated multipliers do not include economic information about social and environmental impacts so that the benefits of mining projects often tend to be over-estimated (see example in Box 1). Indeed, the standard approach for economic impact assessments does not apply readily to social and environmental externalities as social accounting matrices do not record them; i.e. there is no multiplier available to model the social and environmental externalities of a particular intervention.

Box 1 Limitations of a study comparing mining and agriculture scenarios for a proposed gold mine

Source: Integrated Sustainability Services (2013)

Scenario 1: Overall macro-economic impact of proposed gold mine over 50 years on the production, GDP-R, and employment for the primary and secondary study areas

Macro-Economic Impacts of Scenario 1 (50 years; R'000 000, 2012 prices)						
Economic Indicator	Construction phase	Operational phase	Rehabilitation & decommissioning phase	Farm reestablishment phase	Farming	Total
Number of years	2	25	1	5	17	50
Production	14888	23278.0	125.6	140.5	150.5	38583
GDP-R	4978.1	11482.0	62.0	47.0	68.1	16637.1
Employment (numbers per year)	15394	3861	187	58	37	Not applicable

Scenario 2: Overall macro-economic impacts of the current land use (agriculture) over 50 years

Macro-Economic Impacts During Farming (50 years; R'000 000, 2012 prices)				
Economic Indicator	Direct	Indirect	Induced	Total
Production	350	148.3	121.2	619.5
GDP-R	167.1	59.7	53.5	280.3
Employment (numbers per year)	14	6	6	25

The results of this investigation found that Scenario 2 had a much smaller positive economic impact in comparison to Scenario 1. The total economic impact of Scenario 1 far exceeds that of Scenario 2 mainly due the amount of expenditure required to construct, operate and close a large open cast mine.

However, one can argue that the benefits of scenario 1 are over-estimated because there was no information about the costs of environmental and social impacts of the proposed mining project.

Including external costs and benefits in cost–benefit analysis

Using various economic valuation tools and net present value calculations, it is theoretically possible to calculate the net impact of a mining project; i.e. the integrated net economic, social and environmental impact of the proposed scenario(s), expressed in monetary values (Box 2). This would involve assessing the economic value(s) of each positive and/or negative social and environmental impact (externality), which are linked, directly and/or indirectly to stakeholders, at the local, regional, national and/or international level. For instance, these externalities would include those arising from:

▶ Land and soil degradation and pollution, ground and surface water pollution and depletion, air pollution as well as habitat, species and ecosystem loss and destruction

▶ Mining-induced loss and degradation of livelihoods, such as loss or degradation of small scale agriculture, grazing pasture and tourism

▶ Social costs such as increased health care costs and increased family and social breakdown (e.g. divorce, prostitution, child labour, intra- and inter-community conflicts, community–company conflicts)

Box 2 Calculating the net economic impact of a mine

Source: Houdet *et al.* (2014b), adapted from UNEP (2012)

Net economic impact of a proposed mine = mine profitability (A) + external benefits to stakeholders (B) - external costs to society (C) = A + B − C

Mine profitability = A = net present value of revenues - net present value of internal costs

External benefits to stakeholders (positive externalities) = B = sum of net present value of direct, indirect and induced positive economic, social and environmental impacts

External costs to stakeholders (negative externalities) = C = sum of net present value of direct, indirect and induced negative economic, social and environmental impacts

With specific reference to environmental externalities, one may use the total economic value of ecosystems and the associated economic valuation tools to estimate use and non-use values of ecosystems. However, such comprehensive analyzes appear not to be actively pursued by economic impact assessment practitioners in most countries, including South Africa. Only a single case study could be found but there was a lack of transparency on the results (i.e. actual monetary values) and methods used (KPMG, 2014). Beyond the uncomfortable position in which such an approach may put some companies, this could also be explained by the lack of standardized externality valuation methodologies and easily accessible, spatially and time relevant, and inexpensive data sets on both social and environmental impacts, including for ecosystem services. Indeed, the availability and quality of the underlying non-monetary data is of critical importance so as to be able to use robust economic models and generate reliable values.[5]

Mainstreaming ecosystem services valuation in EIA

One may argue that, to mainstream the economic valuation of ecosystem services in a cost-effective manner in EIA processes (i.e. to avoid transaction costs, including for relevant data collection), several issues need to be addressed. First, mining companies, environmental impact assessment practitioners, regulatory bodies and other stakeholders need easy access to detailed and regularly updated spatial and biophysical information about ecosystem services, building on the work undertaken by the South African National Biodiversity Institute on biodiversity mapping and taking it to the next level (i.e. detailed ecosystem services monitoring and mapping, in terms of supply sources and delivery channels and timing to beneficiaries).

Second, sector-specific guidelines for ecosystem services valuation in qualitative, quantitative and economic terms, in different ecosystems/regions and for different types of projects and activities, including different types of mining activities, should be developed. This must be coupled with standardized guidelines and rules for: 1) the drafting of terms of reference for integrating ecosystem services valuation in scoping studies, EIAs, EMPs and closure costing assessments; 2) ensuring that such extended economic impact assessments become mandatory; 3) ensuring that appropriate valuation approaches and tools are used for all relevant assessments (from impact assessment to closure costing) and that all specialist studies provide relevant quantitative biophysical and monetary values of ecosystem services for use by economists as part of their cost–benefit analysis (EIA process) or cost-effectiveness assessment (for EMP) of project alternatives.

---

5 The value of externalities can vary significantly, depending on the economic valuation tool used, quantitative data quality, local site conditions and the changing perceptions of stakeholders. It can also be highly sensitive to changes in interest rates, hence the need for sensitivity analysis of the models (Farrell 2007; UNEP et al., 2012).

Third, the building of an extended national social accounting matrix which would include externality data sets for easy use by all stakeholders should become a priority at the national level. This would allow economic impact assessment practitioners to use externality impact multipliers for each sector and region at different scales, while making sure provisions exist to take into account local contexts, legal aspects and ethical dimensions before making project-specific recommendations.

Conclusion

The 2013 South African Mining and Biodiversity Guidelines are likely to generate further interest in undertaking the valuation of ecosystem services at each step of the mining life-cycle. Yet, further work is needed to clarify how this should be done while applying the impact mitigation hierarchy. This paper has attempted to show that neither non-monetary values nor monetary values of ecosystem services can be the sole basis for decision-making regarding mining project approval. They are complementary values in a broader basket of tools for more sustainable and accountable mining practices. The critical analysis of case studies in this paper has emphasized the need to refer to ethics, stakeholder concerns and needs, policies, laws and regulations as well as international best practices while designing valuation studies and interpreting resulting values in EIA. Specific recommendations on mainstreaming ecosystem services valuation cost-effectively in EIA processes were also proposed, including the development of (and enabling of easy access to) relevant non-monetary and monetary data sets on ecosystem services and the need to standardize terms of reference and methodologies for valuation studies. Such changes would significantly enhance the decision-making capacity of mining companies, regulators and their stakeholders.

References

Baxter, B. (2013). *Updated Wetland Delineation and Assessment for the Proposed Zonnebloem Greenfields Mining Area, Mpumalanga. Final EIA and EMP for the proposed Zonnebloem Opencast Coal Mine*. Golder Associates.

Boyd, J.W., & Banzhaf, S. (2007). What are ecosystem services? The need for standardized environmental accounting units. *Ecological Economics*, 63: 616-626.

Christie, M., Fazey, I., Cooper, R., Hyde, T., & Kenter, J.O. (2012). An evaluation of monetary and non-monetary techniques for assessing the importance of biodiversity and ecosystem services to people in countries with developing economies. *Ecological Economics*, 83: 67-78.

Comello, S.D., Maltais-Landry, G., Schwegler, B.R., & Lepech, M.D. (2014). Firm-level ecosystem service valuation using mechanistic biogeochemical modeling and functional substitutability. *Ecological Economics*, 100: 63-73.

Department of Minerals and Energy (2005). *Guideline document for the evaluation of the quantum of closure-related financial provision provided by a mine.*

Department of Environmental Affairs, Department of Mineral Resources, Chamber of Mines, South African Mining and Biodiversity Forum, & South African National Biodiversity Institute (2013). *Mining and Biodiversity Guideline: Mainstreaming biodiversity into the mining sector.* Pretoria: DEA.

Farrell, K.N. (2007). Living with Living Systems: the co-evolution of values and valuation. *The International Journal of Sustainable Development and World Ecology,* 14(1): 14-26.

FutureWorks (2013). *Ecosystem Services Supply and Demand Assessment for Zonnebloem Coal Mine, Mpumalanga. Final EIA and EMP for the proposed Zonnebloem Opencast Coal Mine.* Golder Associates.

Golder Associates (2009). *Sustainable Development Investigation for NBC: Belfast Project. Exxaro Resources Limited.* Golder Associates.

Haines-Young, R., & Potschin, M. (2013). *CICES V4.3 – Revised report prepared following consultation on CICES Version 4.* EEA Framework Contract No EEA/IEA/09/003.

Houdet, J., & Germaneau, C. (2014). Accounting for biodiversity and ecosystem services from an EMA perspective. Towards a standardised Biodiversity Footprint methodology. In M. Jones (Ed.), *Accounting for biodiversity* (pp. 52-80). London: Routledge.

Houdet, J., Trommetter, M., & Weber, J. (2012). Understanding changes in business strategies regarding biodiversity and ecosystem services. *Ecological Economics,* 73: 37-46.

Houdet, J., Burritt, R., Farrell, K. N., Martin-Ortega, J., Ramin, K., Spurgeon, J., Atkins, J., Steuerman, D., Jones, M., Maleganos, J., Ding, H., Ochieng, C., Naicker, K., Chikozho, C., Finisdore, J., Sukhdev, P. (2014a). *What natural capital disclosure for integrated reporting? Designing and modelling an Integrated Financial – Natural Capital Accounting and Reporting Framework.* Synergiz – ACTS, Working Paper 2014-01.

Houdet, J., Muloopa, H., Ochieng, C., Kutegeka, S., & Nakangu, B. (2014b). *Cost Benefit Analysis of the Mining Sector in Karamoja, Uganda.* IUCN Uganda Country Office: Kampala.

Integrated Sustainability Services (2013). *Economic Impact Assessment of the De Bron-Merriespruit project – Wits Gold.* GCS (Pty) Ltd.

Kelemen, E., García-Llorente, M., Pataki, G., Martín-López, B., & Gómez-Baggethun, E. (2014). Non-monetary techniques for the valuation of ecosystem service. In M. Potschin & K. Jax (Eds.), *OpenNESS Reference Book.* EC FP7 Grant Agreement no. 308428.

Kotze, D.C., Marneweck, G.C., Batchelor, A.L., Lindley, D.S., & Collins, N.B. (2009). *WET-EcoServices: A technique for rapidly assessing ecosystem services supplied by wetlands.* Water Research Commission. WRC TT 339/09.

KPMG (2014). *A new vision of value: Connecting corporate and societal value creation.* KPMG International Cooperative.

Landers, D.H., & Nahlik, A.M. (2013). *Final Ecosystem Goods and Services Classification System (FEGS-CS).* EPA/600/R-13/ORD-004914. US Environmental Protection Agency, Office of Research and Development: Washington, DC.

Levrel, H., Hay, J., Bas, A., Gastineau, P., & Pioch, S. (2012). Coût d'opportunité versus coût du maintien des potentialités écologiques: deux indicateurs économiques pour mesurer les coûts de l'érosion de la biodiversité. *Natures Sciences Sociétés,* 20: 16–29.

McCarthy, T. (2011). The impact of acid mine drainage in South Africa. *South African Journal of Science,* 107(5/6): Art. #712.

Millennium Ecosystem Assessment (2005). *Ecosystems and human wellbeing: synthesis.* World Resources Institute. Island Press: Washington, DC.

Nahlik, A.M., Kentula, M.E., Fennessy, M.S., & Landers, D.H., 2012. Where is the consensus? A proposed foundation for moving ecosystem service concepts into practice. *Ecological Economics,* 77: 27-35.

Natural Capital Coalition (2014). *Valuing natural capital in business. Towards a harmonised protocol.* ICAEW: London.

Ramontja, T., Coetzee, H., & Hobbs, P. J. (2010). *Mine water management in the Witwatersrand Gold Fields with special emphasis on acid mine drainage.* Report to the Inter-Ministerial Committee on Acid Mine Drainage.

Shene-Verdoorn, C.A., & Ncube, N. (2014). *Mining and Biodiversity: Evaluating EAP standards in the sector.* WWF SA.

Swart, J. (2003). Will direct payments help biodiversity? *Science,* 299: 1981.

TEEB (2010). *The Economics of Ecosystems and Biodiversity: Ecological and Economic Foundations.* UNEP/Earthprint: London.

UNEP (2012). *Developing a cost-benefit analysis of mining sites in Mongolia. Annual Report 2011.* Strengthening Environmental Governance in Mongolia, Phase II.

Van Zyl, H., Bond-Smith, M., Minter, T., Botha, M., & Leiman, A. (2012). *Financial Provisions for rehabilitation and closure in South African mining: Discussion document on challenges and recommended improvements.* WWF SA.

Waage, S. (2014). *Making sense of new approaches to business risk and opportunity assessment.* BSR.

Wetland Consulting Services (2013). *Updated wetland delineation and assessment for the proposed Zonnebloem greenfields mining area, Mpumalanga.* Golders Associates.

Thinking
THE
Twenty-First Century

IDEAS FOR THE NEW POLITICAL ECONOMY

MALCOLM McINTOSH

Thinking the Twenty-First Century

Ideas for the New Political Economy

Malcolm McIntosh

- Radical thinking from a pioneer of the corporate responsibility and sustainability movement
- Contextual account of five global changes that will transform a new political economy
- Essential for economists, academics and engaged citizens everywhere

"McIntosh recalls Obama's comment that Nelson Mandela's leadership 'freed the prisoner and jailer'. He explains what we must do to drive the same outcome with tomorrow's economy."

John Elkington, co-founder of Volans and SustainAbility

"This is a powerful work by a man at his peak and will, in fifty years' time, be seen as a masterpiece."

Sir Tim Smit KBE, Executive Chairman, Eden Regeneration, and co-founder of the Eden Project

"This book is both timely and urgent as humanity struggles to seek solutions for a fairer and sustainable future"

Georg Kell, Executive Director, UN Global Compact

In a sophisticated and far-reaching blend of theory and reflection, *Thinking the Twenty-First Century* takes a provocative look at the changes required to build a new global political economy. McIntosh charts five system changes essential to this transition: globality and Earth awareness; the rebalancing of science and awe; peacefulness and the feminization of decision-making; the reorganization of our institutions; and evolution, adaptation and learning. That they are all connected should be obvious, but that they are written about together is less common.

McIntosh argues that these five changes are already under way and need to be accelerated. Combining science, philosophy, politics and economics, *Thinking the Twenty-First Century* questions our current model of capitalism and calls for a much-needed new order. This forceful call to action advocates a balanced political economy with trandisciplinarity, connectivity, accountability and transparency at its centre, as an alternative to a world built on the failing system of neoliberal economics.

From one of the pioneers of the global corporate sustainability and social responsibility movement, this unique book combines analysis, diary and reflection to present a radical way forward for the twenty-first century.

MALCOLM McINTOSH is former Director of the Asia Pacific Centre for Sustainable Enterprise at Griffith University and is now at Bath Spa University. He was previously Special Adviser to the UN Global Compact and is the Founding Editor of the *Journal of Corporate Citizenship*.

Published: April 2015 | **Prices:** ebook: £24.99 | €29.99 | $39.99 | pb: £24.99 | €29.99 | $39.99 | hb: £60.00 | €75.00 | $95.00

DOI: [10.9774/GLEAF.4700.2015.de.00008]

Is Integrated Reporting a Matter of Public Concern?

Evidence from Australia

Patricia T. Strong

University of New South Wales, Australia

The purpose of this study is to critically examine the emergence of integrated reporting as "the" solution to the global criticisms levelled at the inaptness of mandatory corporate and voluntary sustainability reporting. This is considered a matter for public concern as the attempt tries to appease multiple stakeholders whose interests are not aligned. This study adopts an actor–network lens to reveal a holistic view of the integrated reporting development processes in Australia. The study identifies multiple interests and controversies affecting the field, which are theorized using the orders of worth analytical tool to examine controversies that inhibit agreement. Data is gathered through semi-structured interviews, participant observation and a netnographical approach using computer-mediated communication (CMC) tools to access online network sources. Nvivo software is adopted to build a thematic analysis of the interests and controversies. The study reveals that attempts to develop a globally accepted technology have been thwarted by unresolved disputes. The paper concludes that the matter of public concern relates to the expectation of stakeholder inclusiveness but ultimately the development process continues the domination of market interests.

- Sustainability reporting
- Integrated reporting
- Actor–network theory
- Orders of worth
- Netnography

Dr **Patricia T. Strong** is a lecturer at the University of New South Wales. Her research interests include sustainability reporting, integrated reporting, global governance, management accounting practices and accounting education. She teaches in Qualitative Research Methods and E-Business Strategy and Processes and complements her teaching and research interests by her community engagement roles as a company director (MAICD), Community Bank Advisor, Certified Practicing Accountant (CPA) and other philanthropic roles. She worked in industry for 20 years prior to commencing her academic career.

✉ School of Accounting, University of New South Wales, Room 3067, level 3, Quadrangle Building, Kensington Campus, Sydney, NSW 2052, Australia

▢ t.strong@unsw.edu.au

☎ +61 2 9385 6657

CRITICISMS THAT FOCUS ON THE incompleteness of corporate reporting practices and their lack of transparency are not new (Adams, 2004). Extended reporting practices and, in particular, sustainability reporting practices have been proposed as a solution to the dissatisfaction with corporate reporting practices (Gray, 2012). Gray (2010) and Hopwood (2009) have called for researchers to explore the gap between accounting and the sustainability agenda. Recently, there has been a shift globally to address this gap with the emergence of the International Integrated Reporting Council (IIRC) (IIRC, 2011; Adams, 2004).[1] The emergence of this new agenda brings this initiative to the fore as a matter of public concern.

Integrated reporting <IR> offers an alternative to current reporting practices. It presents a company's performance and future prospects based on six capitals (financial, human, intellectual, natural, social and manufactured), in contrast to current practices that usually consist of two separate disconnected reports, the historical financial annual report and the voluntary sustainability report. However, in spite of the accumulating scientific evidence, pertinacious support and a laissez-faire political attitude, sustainability reporting and the more recent <IR> agenda have failed to gain acceptance as part of mainstream financial reporting (Gray, 2010, 2012; Mathews, 1997; Adams et al., 2011).

While tools such as the Global Reporting Initiative (GRI) and triple bottom line (TBL) reporting concepts have been around for decades, they have failed to capture a critical mass of adopters. For example, at a GRI workshop in October 2011, the Australian GRI Focal Point Manager reported that only around 2,000 companies adopted the GRI reporting guidelines and framework in 2010.[2] This is an insignificant number considering the potential number of multinational companies worldwide (Milne and Gray, 2007). The number of <IR> adopters is even lower with only 140 organizations worldwide in 2012 (IIRC, 2013). It seems that despite some level of advancement in reporting practices, very little has been achieved in ensuring accounting for sustainability impacts are incorporated in financial reporting practices (Milne and Gray, 2007; Hopwood, 2009).

A growing interest in <IR> among practitioners and stakeholders has not been matched by research—most research appears as working papers or conference papers (Rowbottom and Locke, 2013; Wild and Van Staden, 2013), although some published articles, such as Cheng et al. (2014) and the *Accounting, Auditing and Accountability Journal* special issue (July 2014) edited by de Villiers et al. (2014), are emerging.

---

1 The IIRC was formed by the convergence of Accounting for Sustainability (A4S) and the Global Reporting Initiative (GRI) with the aim to develop an integrated report <IR>. An overall objective of <IR> is to bring together material information about an organization's strategy, governance, performance and prospects in a way that reflects the commercial, social and environmental context within which it operates (IIRC, Discussion Paper, September, 2011).

2 Information made available by the GRI Focal Point Australia, G4 Public Comment Workshop 13 October 2011, Sydney, Australia.

At the conceptual level <IR> draws together the accounting concepts of accountability, transparency, reporting and financial indicator measurements, with the scientific concepts of climate change impacts, the measurement of non-financial indicators and the hybrid notion of sustainability reporting, politics and power, into one framework. This means that the study of <IR> is complex and multidisciplinary and reaches across jurisdictions. Latour (2004a, p. 4) warns "every time we seek to mix scientific facts with aesthetic, political, economic and moral values, we find ourselves in a quandary". Extending this line of thinking opens up a number of quandaries around the possibility of the coexistence of sustainability issues, moral values, economic rewards and political agendas. In this study, the complexity of this coexistence and how the varying interests and values interconnect, converge and diverge is examined. This paper traces the diverse interests and reveals how they shape the field and how over time stakeholder inclusiveness is reduced as the framework progresses, despite the early illusion of a *shared common goal* (Latour, 2004b).

This paper argues that the IIRC initially claimed a key aim was "to create a globally accepted framework for accounting for sustainability".[3] However more recent announcements and the release of the <IR> framework in December 2013 reveal that the notion of "sustainability" has been reduced in the current IIRC agenda. An IIRC announcement at that time also stated the primary audience of <IR> is the providers of capital and not, as initially proposed, broader stakeholder interests. This is a matter for public concern and this study attempts to reveal "what happened to the sustainability agenda and civic interests" by specifically investigating the issues and challenges arising in the field as different value systems battle to dominate the agenda.

The early integrated reporting literature

As a relatively new phenomenon, <IR> has received limited research attention. At the time of writing this paper much of the research was published in working papers (Rowbottom and Locke, 2013; Wild and Van Staden, 2013). However, published work such as Cheng *et al.* (2014), and the recent studies included in the *Accounting, Auditing and Accountability Journal* special issue (July 2014) edited by de Villiers *et al.* (2014) are now emerging.

The conceptualization of <IR> was the focus of the early <IR> research, followed by some studies of the framework's development process (Adams and Simnett, 2011; Adams *et al.*, 2011; Eccles *et al.*, 2010). A few studies have examined reporting practices in different jurisdictions (Eccles *et al.*, 2010;

---

3 GRI press briefing on the "Formation of the International Integrated Reporting Committee (IIRC)", the Prince's Accounting for Sustainability Project and the Global Reporting Initiative, 2 August 2010, http://www.globalreporting.org/NewsEventsPress/PressResources/ (last accessed 9 August 2010).

Roberts, 2011a, b) and some papers have taken a more critical stance (Gray, 2012; Flower, 2014; Strong, 2014). This early research attempted to provide clarity on what <IR> is and how it will affect accounting, business and audit practices. Eccles *et al.* (2010) conducted one of the earliest studies on <IR> and explored the global landscape prior to the commencement of the framework's development process. The study presented the global collective views of the diverse interests—many of these concerns are still prevalent today. Other studies examined the state of play at the various <IR> development stages, including analysing the discussion paper and consultation draft responses (Gray, 2012; Ioannou and Serafeim, 2011; Adams *et al.*, 2011).

Other key research topics focused on <IR> assurance issues, including what level of assurance, types of services and who should be the providers of the service. Researchers have also studied the potential impact of <IR> and voluntary disclosure practices on the cost of debt (Coram *et al.*, 2009; Cohen *et al.*, 2012; Dhaliwal *et al.*, 2011; Healy and Palepu, 2001). Many researchers have argued <IR> is a research field that requires further investigation (Adams and Simnett, 2011; Adams, 2014; Gray, 2012; de Villiers *et al.*, 2014). However, a key criticism of <IR> research relates to the lack of engagement in the field. This study addresses this gap.

Underlining theoretical deliberations

Considering the complexity of the <IR> landscape, actor–network theory (ANT) offers an appropriate lens for examining the connections between actors and the process of developing a new technology. The term "actor" in ANT terms refers to both human and non-human actants; that is, networks, machines, texts, frameworks, assemblages of practice and dialogue (Pipan and Czarniawska, 2010, p. 224; Latour, 2005, p. 10). Networks are a string of actions, requiring all actors to do something. Actions have effect and translate the events under study. ANT traces the connections and reveals the "traces left behind by some moving agent" (Latour, 2005, p. 132). It reveals the flows of translation, allowing the researchers to capture such movement as the actors are followed *in situ* and events unfold (Robson, 1991, 1992; Callon, 1986).

The concept of translation is important and has been adopted in many ANT inspired accounting research studies, including ethnographic case studies and historical analysis of accounting change-in-action (Miller and O'Leary, 1987; Robson, 1991, 1992; Preston *et al.*, 1992; Chua, 1995). Some researchers extend the notion of translation in a number of contexts such as supply chain management (Briers and Chua, 2001; Chua and Mahama, 2007) and the study of change in the telecommunications sector (Andon *et al.*, 2007). More recently, researchers have proposed new research agendas, methodologies and vocabularies in ANT studies (Justesen and Mouritsen, 2011; Skaerbaek and Tryggestad, 2010; Christensen and Skaerbaek, 2010). Appling this more nuanced approach to ANT studies, this paper extrapolates interests and diverse values around the adoption of <IR> to reveal deeper insights and understandings of controversies surrounding the <IR> agenda (Latour, 2004a, b, 2005).

Christensen and Skaerbaek (2010) adopt a purification process to reveal the introduction of new accounting innovations. Purification refers to "the processes that progress ideas towards acceptance and agreement" (Christensen and Skaerbaek, 2010, p. 525). It seeks to separate facts from values and remove complications. The current study also adopts a purification process to expose tensions and examine them to reveal their effects on <IR> development processes, providing insights into the issues that divide the field and the matters of concern that "keeps controversy alive" in an effort to reveal a richer line of enquiry (Latour, 2004b, p. 103; Justesen and Mouritsen, 2011, p. 183; Christensen and Skaerbaek, 2010).

The previous sections have identified the theoretical lens adopted to study the field and help to build a theorized storyline for this study (Golden-Biddle and Locke, 2007). As a new research domain <IR> has had little attention and there are few empirical studies and even fewer providing a holistic view of interests in the <IR> field. There is little research that examines the matters of concern that divide the field and how such matters are addressed. This study draws attention to the diverse interests and concerns and thus provides deeper insights and understanding of the disputes revolving around the <IR> agenda. By using the ANT lens it enables the research to address this gap by critically investigating attempts to promote the <IR> agenda in Australia. The study focuses on the time frame leading up to the IIRC announcement in 2010 and extends to 2012. Although the study acknowledges the data collection process has continued throughout 2013 as the <IR> development process continued, the extended time period is the subject of a later research study.

Method

The tensions and disputes surrounding the <IR> agenda are examined in this study by taking a holistic perspective of the field. A blended approach to data collection is adopted, spanning a $3\frac{1}{2}$ year netnographical study that adopts computer-mediated communication (CMC) tools to study online communities of practice.[4] This approach is complemented by traditional qualitative data collection methods, such as semi-structured interviews and participant-observation. This includes 34 semi-structured interviews conducted with 13 diverse interest groups accumulating 40 hours of data collection, and participant-observation

---

4 Netnography is the "adaption of qualitative methods utilized with the express aim of enabling a contextually-situated study of virtual communities" (Kozinets, 1998, p. 366). Virtual communities have come to fruition as a consequence of advances in technology and CMC tools. Many <IR> networks adopt CMC tools in their day-to-day activities. Therefore a netnographical approach was vital in this study and the only way the researcher could "make cultural entre to the field" (Kozinets, 2010, p. 61).

at 40 face-to-face communities of practice workshops, briefings and events, accumulating 150 hours of data collection. This holistic approach enables a more comprehensive view of the field, gathering data from multiple sources to provide a form of triangulation and reveal deep insights into the interests and matters of concern affecting the field.

The 3 $^1/_2$ year study was undertaken in three stages. The initial stage began in 2009 and consisted of building a theoretical understanding and knowledge about sustainability reporting practices. Research activities encompassed reviewing the literature and corporate and historical documents available in the public domain, as well as examining corporate and NGO websites and sustainability reports, and participation in online sustainability related discussion forums. The second stage of the study commenced in August 2010 with the announcement of the <IR> agenda and IIRC formation and continued until December 2010. This stage consisted of continued engagement with online communities of practice, conducting four preliminary interviews with key stakeholders and attending nine public briefings. These activities helped to refine the scope of the study. The final stage of the study commenced in January 2011 and continued in an intense capacity until January 2012. During this phase, the researcher engaged in the field almost entirely for one year attending workshops, seminars, briefings, webinar broadcasts and participating in working parties providing commentary to the GRI G4 ongoing development and the <IR> discussion documents and framework development. In this latter stage 25 in-depth semi-structured interviews were conducted.

Table 1 identifies the key interest groups interviewed and the duration of the interview. Most interviews were recorded, excluding four. In those situations the researcher wrote copious notes, typed and distributed them to the interviewee for accuracy and confirmation. Interviewees were promised anonymity therefore participants are identified in generic specialist area terms; that is, accounting or sustainability specialist.

Table 1 <IR> interest groups interviewed

Specialist group	Number of interviews	Duration (hours)
Accounting	7	8.0
Sustainability reporting	4	4.5
Environmental	4	7.0
Accounting academic	4 (1 person interviewed twice)	7.25
Government	1 (2 interviewees)	1.5
Investment community	2	2.25
Civil society, NGO	2	2.0
Company director	1	0.45
Financial institutions	3 (1 with 3 interviewees)	4.0
Labour movement	1	1.0
Sustainability reporter	1	1.0

Specialist group	Number of interviews	Duration (hours)
A4S and IFAC, London	1 (2 interviewees)	1.0
Summary details		
13 specialist groups	31, some had multiple participants; 1 participant was interviewed twice	40.25

The multiple data collection methods and engagement with 13 different specialist interest groups, including attending specialist conferences and workshops, afforded a panoramic view of the matters of concern dividing the field. In some cases, multiple participants from key specialist groups were interviewed and this further enabled the identification, clarification and refinement of key issues.

Data analysis

Interviews were recorded and transcribed into text files and reviewed to ensure completeness and accuracy. Nvivo 9 software, a qualitative data analysis tool, was used to code the data. The text data set was analyzed methodically and systematically to draw inferences and make comparisons and to identify themes (Weber, 1985). Although it is agreed this approach can be subjective, every effort was undertaken not to draw any assumptions or conclusions without supporting data (to triangulate findings) (Lee and Peterson, 1997; Weber, 1985).

During the data collection and analysis stage ongoing hypothesizing and theorizing was a continuous activity until the "best fit between data and analysis" was found (Patton, 1990, p. 462). The coding process resulted in two attempts. In the first attempt all the interviews were coded to expose the key themes and thematic structure. The themes included the interviewee's expertise and background, the changes in practices they identified over their time in the field, their involvement in the various networks shaping sustainability reporting and subsequently <IR>, their concerns relating to the <IR> agenda and speculative comments on the future of <IR>. At this first attempt to analysis the data, too much minute detail was revealed, which hampered any cohesive conclusions. Although it did reveal some insights that supported some claims in the literature. Thus a second phase of coding analysis was undertaken.

In this analysis, underpinning values held by the interests were revealed that enabled categorization of the interest groups using Boltanski and Thevenot's (1999, 2006) orders of worth framing. This provided better theorizing of the diverse interests and revealed a more collective and cohesive view of the field, yet still exposing diverse motives and agendas. In brief, the most pertinent orders of worth framing applicable to this study are *market, industrial* and *civic* interests. *Market* interests tend to be motivated by monetary rewards, self-interest and upholding capitalist traditions. *Industrial* interests tend to focus on productivity and efficiency and the tools, resources and frameworks that promote productivity goals. However, it is acknowledged these *industrial* goals are also generally supportive of capitalist ideals and may be underpinned by market self-interest.

Civic interests on the other hand tend to relate to collective interests and the pursuit of "the greater good for society". These include issues such as equality, environmental preservation and sustainable development and human rights concerns for all communities. Boltanski and Thevenot (1999, 2006) discuss other values but those are less relevant to this study.[5]

Adopting the orders of worth framing facilitates building a deeper level of understanding of the interests that divide actors and their underlying values and justifications that ultimately inhibit consensus. This more cohesive and collective analysis highlighted the multiplicity of interests and agendas. The next section will illustrate how the orders of worth framing have been applied to actors, and also illustrates the different interests and agendas.

Integrated reporting in Australia

In this section the unique Australian <IR> story is presented revealing key local and global influences that shape the newly emerging <IR> framework. The actors and the issues that cause them concern are examined. The story reveals the state of play in the Australian sustainability reporting field and its state of readiness for reporting change prior to the IIRC announcement in August 2010 and the subsequent <IR> journey.

Reporting on sustainability type issues and impacts has been a matter of concern in Australia for some time, particularly for civic interest groups attempting to build a critical mass in reporting practices. Various legislative and regulatory initiatives have increased the corporate reporting burden, such as climate change legislation, the Energy Efficiency Act 2006, the National Greenhouse Gas Emissions Scheme 2007 and other changes in corporate reporting requirements as a result of environmental, social and governance issues.

Sustainability has not always been the term adopted to refer to these extended reporting practices. The accounting literature and interview data reveal that various terms have been coined over time, including: environmental, social, and corporate social responsibility (CSR) or triple bottom line (TBL) reporting. However, "sustainability" became the label in the 21st century and later this was replaced by environmental, social and governance (ESG) reporting. The following quotes provide a sense of how the language changed over time.

---

5 Orders of worth framing provides a theorization tool with regimes of justification framed by six distinct world views as a way of making sense of the diverse interests embroiled in any dispute (Boltantski and Thevenot, 1999, 2006). The six values are: *market, industrial, civic, inspired, domestic* and *renowned*. Inspired relates to the world of artists whose worth is independent of the opinions of others; domestic refers to a world where the actors' values stem from their position in the community, society or family. In this regime power is drawn from an authority position and protection and support is granted in return for respect, loyalty and allegiance. In the renowned value system actors are valued if they are famous, a celebrity or opinion leader. These last three classifications are less relevant to this <IR> study.

So it's corporate sustainability policy or CSR or whatever was the most recent term at that time. The names change as we progress over time (Environmental Specialist 2).

There was always frustration about not having enough disclosure or information on corporate performance in sustainability or sustainable development as it was called then (Environmental Specialist 3).

Other significant events include the Australian Government's launch of a Parliamentary Joint Committee (PJC) inquiry into "Corporate Responsibility: Managing Risk and Creating Value". The PJC recommended sustainability reporting practices remain voluntary. However, sustainability reporting supporters tend to view the PJC inquiry as a "significant turning point" in Australia as it raised sustainability reporting issues as a *matter of public concern* in the attention of the Australian public. As one financial community expert states: "We released what was at the time a landmark parliamentary enquiry on corporate responsibility. It gelled with a lot of the reporters about the barriers to the uptake of ESG by corporations and financial markets" (Investment Community Specialist 2).

An additional outcome of this PJC inquiry was the funding by the Australian Government of the Saint James Ethics Centre (SJEC) to establish "The Hub" of responsible business practices and the GRI and the UNGC Focal Points in Australia. This ultimately created a highly organized proactive civic interest network in Australia, which continues to collaborate and contribute to other key networks to ensure that the civic voice is heard in the <IR> space. This discussion now considers the other actors assembled around this agenda and their orders of worth.

The orders of worth values most pertinent to this study have been adopted to classify actors into collectives that appear to share common motives and interests (Boltanski and Thevenot, 1999, 2006). Table 2 presents the actors and their underpinning values. The first column identifies the orders of worth value that appears to be espoused by the actor, the second column groups the actors that appear to share this value together. The third column suggests an underlying value or motive that underpins the actors' actions. The last column provides exemplar quotes illustrating the proposed underlying motive that may be hidden and contrary to their initial motive.

It is, however, important to emphasize that although each actor may have an espoused predominant value and several actors have been grouped together under a single value, there is *no* suggestion that these actors are a united cohesive collective. Each actor has their own agenda and motivation, and these may not cohesively align with the others in the groupings. For example, company directors and the investment community both undoubtedly hold *market* values. But their individual motives may vary depending on their long-term or short-term goals.

The *industrial* motivated network provides a further example related to underlying motive. The IIRC, A4S, and the Australian-based Business Reporters Leaders Forum (BRLF) espouse *industrial* values to improve reporting tools. However, many of their respective constituencies stand to gain financially should the framework be accepted as the marketplace for assurance, accounting and other advisory services will increase. It would be naïve to ignore these other underlying market motives.

Table 2 Orders of worth values and actors in the <IR> field

Key value	Actors	Underlying motives	Exemplar quotes
Market: Pursuit of profits, self-interest, monetary returns	Accounting profession: CPA, ICAA, Big 4 accounting firms Directors: AICD and G100 CFOs Investment community	Overall market growth Expanding the assurance and services field Maximize ROIs, incentives and rewards	"Integrated reporting is a potentially big revenue stream for the accounting profession" (Government Specialist) "It's clear as daylight that there's a massive business interest involved for the accounting firms" (Labour Specialist) "Individuals are rewarded on their financial ROI decisions based on very short-term financial performance, to bring in risk and financial implications over a longer timeframe will require huge structural changes" (Investment Specialist)
Industrial: To improve reporting tools, frameworks technologies	IIRC A4S IFAC Regulators Business Reporting Leaders Forum (BRLF)	The quotes support industrial interests but these networks also stand to gain financial rewards from an expanded assurance market	"The IIRC aims to forge a globally accepted framework", "a framework fit for purpose in the 21st century" (IIRC DP, 2011, pp. 7, 9) "IFAC's overall aim is to promote a standardized frameworks" (IFAC website) "A goal of A4S is to provide practical guidelines and tools; to develop systems to assist organizations; to provide reporting models" (A4S)
Civic: Greater good for society and collective interests	GRI, UNGC, and SJEC Sustainability specialists Human rights, social and community Environment specialists Government	Many of these networks hold genuine altruistic values and/or special interests in human rights, environmental, climate change and social impacts. But it is naïve to think they have no market interests	"The GRI is about collaborating together, a consensus seeking process ... providing a forum for diverse views ... building a multi stakeholder approach" (3 quotes from different Environmental Specialists) "Both the GRI and UNGC networks operate to promote the greater good. The GRI operationalizes the 10 UN universal principles, i.e. human rights, labour, environmental and anti-corruption practices underpin many GRI KPIs" (NGO Specialist)

It is important to note that the very meaning of an <IR> framework and the language underpinning it is likely to denote different things to different interest groups. Motives and values depend on the actors' overall specialist concern, such as environmental, social and community, labour and human rights, or market. Such interests may not translate or align with others in the collective. Table 2 gathers together groups of actors representing collective interests, yet it also reveals evidence of conflicting motives between actors' behaviours and espoused values.

For example, one of IFAC's[6] goals is to "adopt international standards and guidance". Once again this emphasizes a strong industrial focus. However, another IFAC goal is to "contribute to the development of strong professional accountancy organizations", which clearly indicates *market* values may also underpin IFAC's motivation to be involved in the development of <IR>.

If the accounting bodies and the Big 4 accounting firms are examined carefully, it is clear that market interests are considered as the predominant value as illustrated in the quotes in Table 2. The Big 4 accounting firms participate in a number of collaborative arrangements to improve accounting technologies, signalling a clear industrial value. However, as the quotes in the table argue, other interest groups speculate this is driven by the desire to gain a competitive advantage and for the accounting profession to dominate the assurance services marketplace.

As noted, it is clear that company directors and the investment community are also driven by *market* interests. However, tensions exist in relation to the timing of investment returns. Many within the investment community are focused on short-term returns, whereas company directors may consider a longer-term view of their return on investment.

Although there is an appearance that initial espoused motives may align, and this facilitates building artificial collectives for data analysis purposes, these alignments may be fragile as the groups do not all share the same language, meaning and motivation. An illustration of this ambiguity and lack of shared meaning was evident through the IIRC Discussion Paper (DP) response analysis (IIRC, 2012). This revealed confusion and ambiguity around the terms purported in the DP. For example, question 5 asked about "value"; respondents questioned "value to whom?" indicating a lack of shared understanding about the fundamentals and the language. Further contentious issues as the <IR> agenda forged ahead are now discussed.

Contests and collisions on the path to integrated reporting

From the very beginning, at the international <IR> committee announcement in Sydney on 9 August 2010, there were overt signs of tension as illustrated in the researcher's journal notes drafted that day.

---

6 International Federation of Accountants (IFAC) website: http://www.ifac.org/about-ifac (last accessed 27/05/12).

> We were waiting for a press announcement. There was an air of excitement as we all realized something was afoot. The Global Reporting Initiative (GRI) had converged with the Accounting for Sustainability (A4S) project to lead an integrated reporting agenda. Many in the room were not happy about the future prospects of this alliance. An intense debate unfolded...

Key concerns from the sustainability and environmental perspectives related to the fear that any gains that had been achieved in the sustainability space over the previous decades would be lost. Some GRI supporters felt the future existence of the GRI was threatened and there was deep scepticism around the motives of the accounting fraternity in their support for an integrated report.

Other tensions related to market interests and the challenges of accommodating the shift to an <IR> agenda. These were discussed several times in interviews for this study and revealed in the following quote.

> Being competitive in a capital market is obviously what drives the markets, changing that mentality is the key challenge. The other major challenge is the short termism in terms of annual versus three to five year returns, whether it's performance bonuses, CEOs or fund managers, these things basically define how capital markets work. It is driven by monetary reward (Accounting Specialist 3).

Further tensions were acknowledged by an NGO leader who pointed out that NGOs and environmental movements are at odds with the <IR> agenda and in particular the notion of *human capital*.

> People from NGOs and the environmental movement and all sorts of others are worried that any attempts to try and reduce to things where they can be calculated on the basis of price might in some sense diminish the quality of recognition for what they're trying to promote (NGO Leader 1).

> Do we really want to call it *human capital* or does that just reduce people to being just another set of things to be counted? (NGO Leader 1, emphasis added to reflect the speaker's tone)

These quotes provide a flavour of some of the very early tensions in the field. As the <IR> journey progressed, many of the issues that divided interests became more apparent. An analysis of a survey of issues impacting diverse interest groups in the Australian context was undertaken by the Business Reporting Leaders Forum (BRLF), and presented in February 2011. Figure 1 shows an analysis of the key interest groups' issues and provides an overview of converging and diverging interests and issues dividing the key Australian interest groups at that time.

Figure 1 Diverse interests and key issues

Source: Strong (2014, p. 162); figure created from data collected from BRLF commissioned research and tabled at BRLF meeting 4 February 2011

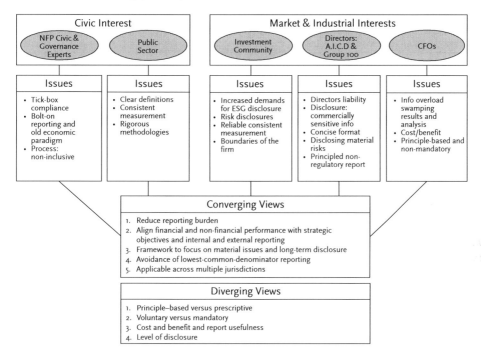

By the time the <IR> discussion paper submissions were analyzed and presented in July 2012, the issues that still divided interests revolved around three key themes. The first related to the *purpose and format* of the reports. The second revolved around the *content and terms* adopted in the proposed framework and the third related to the controversy concerning *the role of the regulator* and *mandatory versus voluntary* reporting practices. These issues appear to be fundamental matters of concern that still divide interests. It is these fundamental issues and matters of public concern where even the language adopted is ambiguous and such disputes still continue.

Discussion

In summary, <IR> was initially greeted with high expectations, or as an investment community specialist suggested, it was "the great white hope". Gray (2012) refers to the "nirvana" of reporting. The IIRC announcement mobilized a wide cross-section of key actors, including the accounting fraternity, regulators, corporate Australia, some government interests and civic interest groups including NGO leaders, environmental, human rights and labour movement specialists. Specific networks emerged including the IIRC and the BRLF with a key objective to mobilize Australian constituencies to support <IR>.

However, over time fractures appeared in the networks surrounding <IR>. For example, directors had concerns about their liability and the disclosure of company-sensitive information. They demonstrated their resistance to <IR> by failing to endorse the final framework that was released in December 2013. At the time of writing this paper these issues are still unresolved and Australian company directors still regard <IR> as a matter for public concern.

Disputes also continue around the *content and format* of the reports and the nature of non-financial indicators and the disclosure of information. These unresolved matters of concern led to civic interests and sustainability issues in general being side-lined or crowded out. It would seem the GRI Organizational Stakeholder Network's initial fear of the reporting agenda being hijacked by the accounting specialists has come to fruition. These early matter of concern have now been addressed and this is perhaps to the detriment of the sustainability agenda. The December 2013 IIRC announcements finally declared the ultimate audience for the integrated report is the providers of capital. <IR> does not replace any current mandated corporate reporting requirements nor reduce the reporting burden. It is unequivocal now too that <IR> does not replace any sustainability reporting tools and specifically not the GRI, so what has happened to the sustainability reporting agenda?

The findings as identified in the empirical section above support the ideas in the recent diffusion literature that the introduction of a new accounting technology is not linear but instead generally exhibits multiple beginnings and abandonments and tends to grow gradually (Malmi, 1999; Jones and Dugdale, 2002; Bol and Moers, 2010). This is particularly apt in the study of the sustainability reporting journey and the many different and separate labels and reporting technologies that preceded <IR>. This is in addition to the analysis of the low adoption rates for the GRI, considering it is the most popular sustainability reporting tool and has been around for over a decade (Gray, 2010). The <IR> journey appears to follow a similar trajectory with only 75 businesses adopting it in the first year of its pilot programme and 140 in the second year, 2013.[7] While the low adoption rates may be due to <IR> being in the early stages of the adoption life cycle, these rates are still very low considering the initial global interests mobilized (Gray, 2012; Gray and Milne, 2004).[8]

From the regulatory perspective and in the context of the mandatory–voluntary reporting debate, it seems as if global actors are waiting to learn from the early pioneers, including South Africa, and their experience with regulatory support for <IR> practices since 2010 (King and Roberts, 2013). However, many countries seem reluctant to take such a strong governmental stand (Lapsley and Wright, 2004).

The accounting literature also advises the diffusion of new technologies tends to be affected by more than just economic forces or rational choice decisions.

---

7 The figures are quoted from the IIRC Pilot Program 2012 Year Book and 2013 Year Book. Refer to http://www.theiirc.org/resources-2/other-publications/2012-yearbook/ and http://www.theiirc.org/companies-and-investors/ (last accessed 30 June 2014).

8 Refer to the IIRC website: http://examples.theiirc.org/home (last accessed 30 June 2014).

Generally, political actors and social factors often influence the acceptance process, including the enrolment of powerful actors and allies to provide institutional legitimacy for the new technology (Chua and Taylor, 2008; Qu and Cooper, 2011; Lapsley and Wright, 2004). In the <IR> journey several powerful actors and allies combined forces to advance the <IR> agenda. For example, the IIRC formation resulted from the convergence of two distinct influential actors, A4S and the GRI, representing two diverging interest groups, one predominately accounting based (A4S) and the other sustainability focused (GRI). This new network (the IIRC) enrolled many other significant actors and political interests to further its agenda, such as IFAC, regulatory regimes, the accounting bodies and the investor community network. However, there is speculation that the newly formed networks have not entirely resolved their outstanding matters of concern despite mobilizing powerful allies and their respective constituencies to embrace the <IR> agenda. As the journey progressed some groups appear to have withdrawn from the debate as their interests were no longer being served. It is important to have the right stakeholders involved in the processes of shaping the new framework as this adds to the legitimacy of the activity (Qu and Cooper, 2011). Where were all the stakeholders assembled and did they have influence in the <IR> developmental process? Did all stakeholders have an equal voice and were all the voices heard? It seems not; as the process continued it became less stakeholder inclusive.

The adoption of the orders of worth framing has facilitated the identification of the actors assembled in the <IR> field and the diverse interests and matters of concern that separate interests and reveal underlying unresolved issues. The ANT lens has facilitated the gathering of data from a holistic perspective, which enabled this study to make a contribution to two streams of literature. First, an extension to the sustainability literature as <IR> may be deemed a new chapter in the sustainability literature; and second, the integrated reporting literature by providing an empirical holistic study of the early issues impacting the <IR> journey.

Conclusion

The <IR> agenda is an important matter of public concern as it impacts many interest groups. Those interests include *market*, such as company directors and the investment community who were dissatisfied with corporate reporting and its lack of transparency and had major concerns about an increasing corporate reporting burden. There was hope that <IR> would solve many of these concerns. Civic interest groups also hoped that <IR> would legitimize voluntary sustainability reporting and increase adoption rates. There was even a notion that <IR> practices would finally bring sustainability reporting "in from the cold" (Parker, 2005) and that such practices would be accepted into mainstream accounting reports (Gray, 2001; Adams, 2004) and promised the "nirvana" in corporate reporting (Gray, 2012).

The diverse interest groups (market, industrial and civic) surrounding the emerging innovation, scrambled to influence the new framework in the expectation their interests would be served by the <IR> agenda (Latour, 2005; Boltanski and Thevenot, 1999, 2006). However, as the refinement of the framework progressed, broader stakeholder interests were reduced, for example, civic interests appear to be side-lined as the more dominant market interests appear to have been reinforced. This reduction of broader public interest voices is a matter of public concern.

These contentious matters of concern were reinforced by the shifting agenda, as the framework was further refined and the target audience was announced and civic interests appeared to be reduced in the <IR> agenda. I speculate that the GRI, realizing that <IR> was not going to meet sustainability reporters' expectations and address sustainability reporting needs, decided to fill the gap in this space. The GRI continued its own developmental journey to maintain relevance to its multiple constituencies and produced a G4 version of its framework and guidelines.

Clearly, as the <IR> journey continues and further refinement takes place, matters of concern around content and format of the report and the voluntary–mandatory governance debate will hopefully be addressed. At this stage researchers argue about the success or failure of the new reporting technology, although some say it is too soon to call (Flower, 2014; Adams, 2014). Many researchers claim <IR> is an under-researched phenomenon and call for further research (Gray, 2012; de Villiers *et al.*, 2014). But what is certain is that <IR> has travelled a contentious journey to date and will continue to be a challenging issue of public concern for some time to come.

Contribution, limitations and future research directions

This research contributes to the <IR> literature by providing empirical evidence revealing a comprehensive view of <IR> as the journey unfolds. The adoption of the orders of worth framing (Boltanski and Thevenot, 1999, 2006) helps capture the controversies, activities and interests before everything is "black boxed" (Latour, 1987, 2005). This analysis provides deeper insights and understanding of the disputes and interests that surround the agenda.

The research does, however, have some limitations. First, the timeframe for the study mainly concentrates on the period between 2010 and the end of 2012, although a cursory overview of 2013 has been included to provide a more complete view of the <IR> development process and the release of the final framework. Second, it is limited by the generic criticisms related to reliability and validity associated with qualitative field research and third by the established restrictions associated with non-face-to-face interactions in a netnographical study (Ahrens and Chapman, 2006; Kozinets, 2010). However, the researcher has attempted to mitigate these limitations by collecting multiple sources of data including interviews from different perspectives around the same issue, reviewing and reflecting on field notes and conducting critical discussions with other researchers and key actors in the field, thus presenting a more comprehensive view of the data and adopting the process of "plausible fit" between the problem, the theory and the data (Ahrens and Chapman, 2006, p. 836). The researcher continues to collect data from the field and the extended period will be the subject of another paper.

This <IR> research field offers many opportunities to undertake research at different levels of analysis, including individual, firm, industry or country. There are also opportunities to undertake further research into implementation and embedding practices, and comparative studies between organizations, across industries or countries and international studies across multiple jurisdictions and different regulatory approaches.

In concluding, <IR> offers a lucrative field for future research as a new phenomenon and academics, researchers and practitioners are all interested in how this new framework will affect and effect their interests. This paper contributes to these communities by providing insights into the many diverging interests, underlying issues and disputes still evident in the field. The ANT lens exposes the complexity and interconnections in the web of relations and the conditions affecting their interests. The orders of worth framing provide a useful diagnostic tool to better theorize and understand the resistance in the <IR> field or in any dispute situation. This paper contributes to both the sustainability and integrated reporting literatures by extending our knowledge of practices and interests influencing this new phenomenon and revealing an emerging historical journey.

Bibliography

Adams, C. A. (2004). The ethical, social and environmental reporting performance portrayal gap. *Accounting, Auditing and Accountability Journal*, 17(5), 731-757.

Adams, C. (2014). The international integrated reporting council: A call to action. *Critical Perspectives on Accounting*, doi: 10.1016/j.cpa.2014.07.001

Adams, S., & Simnett, R. (2011). Integrated Reporting: An opportunity for Australia's not-for-profit sector. *Australian Accounting Review*, 21(3), 292-301.

Adams, S., Fries, J., & Simnett, R. (2011). The journey towards integrated reporting. *Accountants' Digest*, 558 (May), 1-45.

Ahrens, T., & Chapman, C.S. (2006). Doing qualitative field research in management accounting: Positioning data to contribute to theory. *Accounting, Organizations and Society*, 31(8), 819-841.

Andon, P., Baxter, J., & Chua, W.F. (2007). Accounting change as relational drifting: A field study of experiments with performance measurement. *Management Accounting Research*, 18(2), 273-308.

Bol, J.C., & Moers, F. (2010). The dynamics of incentive contracting: The role of learning in the diffusion process. *Accounting, Organizations and Society*, 35: 721-736.

Boltanski, L., & Thevenot, L. (1999). The sociology of critical capacity. *European Journal of Social Theory*, 2(3), 359-377.

Boltanski, L., & Thevenot, L. (2006). *On Justification: Economies of Worth* (C. Porter translator). Oxfordshire: Princeton University Press.

Briers, M., & Chua, W.F. (2001). The role of actor–networks and boundary objects in management accounting change: A field study of an implementation of activity-based costing. *Accounting, Organizations and Society*, 26(3), 237-269.

Callon, M. (1986). Some elements of a sociology of translation domestication of the scallops and the fishermen of St Brieux Bay. In J. Law (Ed), *Power, Action and Belief: A New Sociology of Knowledge?* (pp. 196-229). Boston: Routledge.

Cheng, M., Green, W., Conradie, P., Konishi, N., & Romi, A. (2014). The international integrated reporting framework: Key issues and future research opportunities. *Journal of International Financial Management & Accounting*, 25(1), 90-119.

Christensen, M., & Skaerbaek, P. (2010). Consultancy outputs and the purification of accounting technologies. *Accounting, Organizations and Society*, 35(5), 524-545.

Chua, W.F. (1995). Experts, networks and inscriptions in the fabrication of accounting images: A story of representation of three public hospitals. *Accounting, Organizations and Society*, 20(2-3), 111-145.

Chua, W.F., & Mahama, H. (2007). The effect of network ties on accounting controls in a supply alliance: Field study evidence. *Contemporary Accounting Research*, 24(1), 47-86.

Chua, W.F., & Taylor, S.L. (2008). The rise and rise of IFRS: An examination of IFRS diffusion. *Journal of Accounting and Public Policy*, 27(6), 462-473.

Cohen, J., Holder-Webb, L., Nath, L., & Wood, D. (2012). Corporate reporting on non-financial leading indicators of economic performance and sustainability. *Accounting Horizons*, 26(1), 65-90.

Coram, P.J., Monroe, G.S., & Woodliff, D.R. (2009). The value of assurance on voluntary non-financial disclosure: An experimental evaluation. *Auditing: A Journal of Practice and Theory*, March: 137-151.

De Villers, C., Rinaldi, L., & Unerman, J. (2014). Integrated reporting: Insights, gaps and an agenda for future research. *Accounting, Auditing and Accountability Journal*, 27(7), 1042-1067.

Dhaliwal, D., Zhen, L., Tsang, A., & George, Y. (2011). Voluntary non-financial disclosure and the cost of equity capital: The initiation of corporate social responsibility reporting. *The Accounting Review*, 87(3), 723-760.

Eccles, R.G., Cheng, B., & Saltzman, D. (2010). *The Landscape of Integrated Reporting: Reflections and Next Steps*. Harvard Business School, e-book.

Flower, J. (2014). The Internal Integrated Reporting Council: A story of failure. *Critical Perspectives on Accounting*, doi: 10.1016/j.cpa.2014.07.002.

Golden-Biddle, K., & Locke, K. (2007). *Composing Qualitative Research: Crafting a Theorized Storyline*. Sage Research Methods, Chap 2, pp. 26-47.

Gray, R. (2001). Thirty years of social accounting, reporting and auditing: What (if anything) have we learnt? *Business Ethics: A European Review*, 10(1), 9-15.

Gray, R. (2010). Is accounting for sustainability actually accounting for sustainability…and how would we know? An exploration of narratives of organizations and the planet. *Accounting Organizations and Society*, 35(1), 47-62.

Gray, R. H. (2012). 'Integrated Reporting: Integrated with what and for whom?' *The Loop*, 5.

Gray, R., & Milne, M. (2004). Towards reporting on the triple bottom line: Mirage, methods and myths. In A. Henriques, & J. Richardson (Eds.), *Triple Bottom Line: Does It All Add up?* (pp. 70-80). London: Earthscan.

GRI (Global Reporting Initiative) (2010). *Formation of the International Integrated Reporting Committee (IIRC)*, The Prince's Accounting For Sustainability Project and The Global Reporting Initiative, 2nd August 2010, press release. Retrieved from http://www.global-reporting.org/NewsEventsPress/PressResources.

Healy, P.M., & Palepu, K.G. (2001). Information asymmetry, corporate disclosure, and the capital markets: A review of the empirical disclosure literature. *Journal of Accounting and Economics*, 31, 405-440.

Hopwood, A.G. (2009). Accounting and the environment. *Accounting, Organizations and Society*, 34(3-4), 433-439.

IIRC (International Integrated Reporting Committee) (2011). *Towards Integrated Reporting: Communicating Value in the 21st Century,* Discussion Paper. Retrieved from http://www.theiirc.org.

IIRC (International Integrated Reporting Council) (2012), *Towards Integrated Reporting: Communicating Value in the 21st Century,* Summary to the September 2011 Discussion Paper and Next Steps. Retrieved from http://www.theiirc.org.

IIRC (International Integrated Reporting Council) (2013). Integrated Reporting Framework. Retrieved from http://www.theiirc.org/wp-content/uploads/2013/12/13-12-08-THE-INTERNATIONAL-IR-FRAMEWORK-2-1.pdf.

Ioannou, I., & Serafeim, G. (2011). *The Consequences of Mandatory Corporate Sustainability Reporting.* Harvard Business School Working Paper 11-100.

Jones, T.C., & Dugdale, D. (2002). The ABC bandwagon and the juggernaut of modernity. *Accounting, Organizations and Society,* 37, 121-163.

Justesen, L., & Mouritsen, J. (2011). Effects of actor–network theory in accounting research. *Accounting, Auditing and Accountability Journal,* 24(2), 161-193.

King, M., & Roberts, L. (2013). *Integrate Doing Business in the 21st Century.* Cape Town: Juta & Company Ltd.

Kozinets, R.V. (1998). On netnography: Initial reflections on consumer research investigations of cyberculture. *Advances in Consumer Research,* 25(1), 366-371.

Kozinets, R.V. (2010). *Netnography: Doing Ethnographic Research Online.* London: Sage.

Lapsley, I., & Wright, E. (2004). The diffusion of management accounting innovations in the public sector: A research agenda. *Management Accounting Research,* 15(3), 355-374.

Latour, B. (1987). *Science in Action.* Cambridge MA: Harvard University Press.

Latour, B. (2004a). *Politics of Nature: How to Bring the Sciences into Democracy.* Cambridge, MA: Harvard University Press.

Latour, B. (2004b). Why has critique run out of steam? From matters of fact to matters of concern. *Critical Inquiry,* 30(Winter), 225-248.

Latour, B. (2005). *Reassembling the Social.* Oxford: Oxford University Press.

Lee, F., & Peterson, C. (1997). Content analysis of archival data. *Journal of Consulting and Clinical Psychology,* 65(6), 959-969.

Malmi, T. (1999). Activity-based costing diffusion across organizations: An exploratory empirical analysis of Finnish firms. *Accounting, Organizations and Society,* 24(8), 649-672.

Mathews, M.R. (1997). Twenty-five years of social and environmental accounting research: Is there a silver jubilee to celebrate? *Accounting, Auditing and Accountability Journal,* 10(4), 481-531.

Miller, P., & O'Leary, T. (1987). Accounting and the construction of the governable person. *Accounting, Organizations and Society,* 12(3), 235-265.

Milne, M., & Gray, R. (2007). Future prospects for corporate sustainability reporting. In J. Unerman, J. Bebbington, & B. O'Dwyer (Eds.). *Sustainability Accounting and Accountability* (pp. 184-207). Oxford: Routledge.

Parker, L.D. (2005). Social and environmental accountability research: A view from the commentary box. *Accounting, Auditing and Accountability Journal,* 18(6), 842-860.

Patton, M.Q. (1990). *Qualitative Evaluation and Research Methods.* California: Sage.

Pipan, T., & Czarniawska, B. (2010). How to construct an actor–network: Management accounting from idea to practice. *Critical Perspectives on Accounting,* 21(3), 243-251.

Preston, A., Cooper, D.J., & Coombs, R.W. (1992). Fabricating budgets: A study of the production of management budgeting in the National Health Service. *Accounting, Organizations and Society,* 17(6), 561-593.

Qu, S.Q., & Cooper, D.J. (2011). The role of inscription in producing a balanced scorecard. *Accounting, Organizations and Society,* 26, 344-362.

Roberts, L. (2011a). Integrated Reporting: The status quo. *Accountancy SA,* December, 11-12.

Roberts, L. (2011b). South Africa's early reporters: Not yet an ideal landscape. *Accountancy SA*, December/January, 22-23.

Robson, K. (1991). On the arenas of accounting change: The process of translation. *Accounting, Organizations and Society*, 16 (5-6), 547-570.

Robson, K. (1992). Accounting numbers as 'Inscription': Action at a distance and the development of accounting. *Accounting, Organizations and Society*, 17(7), 685-708.

Rowbottom, N., & Locke, J. (2013). The emergence of integrated reporting. Paper presented at the *Seventh Asia Pacific Interdisciplinary Research in Accounting (APIRA) Conference*, Kobe, Japan, 26–28 July 2013.

Skaerbaek, P., & Tryggestad, K. (2010). The role of accounting devices in performing corporate strategy. *Accounting, Organizations and Society*, 35(1), 108-124.

Strong, P.T. (2014). *Integrated Reporting in Australia: A Study of Key Interests and Effects*. PhD Thesis, University of New South Wales. http://www.unsworks.unsw.edu.au/primo_library/libweb/action/dlDisplay.do?vid=UNSWORKS&docId=unsworks_11990.

Weber, R.P. (1985). *Basic Content Analysis*. California: Sage.

Wild, S., & Van Staden, C. (2013). Integrated Reporting: Initial analysis of early reporters—An institutional theory approach. Paper presented at the *Asia Pacific Interdisciplinary Research in Accounting (APIRA) Conference*, Kobe, Japan, 26–28 July 2013.

DOI: [10.9774/GLEAF.4700.2015.de.00009]

Chief Mohlomi

A Pioneer in Bridging Knowledge from Enterprises of Science, Business and Politics in Southern Africa in the 18th Century

Khali Mofuoa

Charles Sturt University, Australia

The growth and specialization in knowledge production from enterprises of knowledge in the 20th century has led to a major diffraction of the intellectual terrain and a growing distance between knowledge boundaries. It is in this regard that the need to build bridges between various sources of knowledge has become more urgent than ever before. Is this gap worth filling? The answer is a resounding, yes, for a variety of reasons from a responsible leadership viewpoint: first, to generate understanding of leadership responsibilities needed for human progress and development between and across enterprises of knowledge; and second, to create a dialogue about crucial multi-disciplinary insights and knowledge needed to tackle complex development issues facing humanity. Drawing on lessons largely from southern Africa in the 18th century, the paper presents Chief Mohlomi as a pioneer in applying a unity of knowledge approach regarding the enterprise of science, business and of politics for human progress and development. The chief led and set in motion what McIntosh (2013) dubbed "the necessary transition" for transformative change towards a just and sustainable southern Africa during the 18th century.

- Chief Mohlomi and Moshoeshoe
- Basotho of Lesotho
- Responsible leadership
- Knowledge sources and enterprises
- Human progress and development
- Southern Africa

Khali is currently a long-distance PhD student at the Centre for Applied Philosophy and Public Ethics, Charles Stuart University (Australia). He is a former assistant lecturer/research assistant in applied ethics at St Augustine College of South Africa, and a former lecturer in Political and Administrative Studies at the National University of Lesotho. Khali holds an MPhil in Applied Ethics from the University of Stellenbosch (South Africa); a Master's degree in Public Sector Management from the University of the West Indies (Jamaica); a Post-Graduate Diploma in Law from the Universities of Cape Town (South Africa), Namibia and Lesotho; and a Bachelor of Arts in Political Science and Public Administration from the National University of Lesotho.

✉ Centre for Applied Philosophy and Public Ethics, Charles Stuart University, Level 1, Brisbane Avenue, Barton ACT 2600, Australia

Active address:
PO Box 2283, Lonehill, 2062, South Africa

🖳 khalimo25@gmail.com

O UR INCREASINGLY INTERCONNECTED AND COMPLEX world filled with an abundance of evolving knowledge presents us with growing conundrums. Today, the enterprises of science, business and politics form global sources of knowledge "fueled by billions of dollars and driven by a growing army of researchers" (Clough, 2011, p. 46). In this regard, Clough (2011, p. 46) writes,

> Our ability to survive as a society depends in large part on the innovations brought about by *these enterprises as sources of knowledge,* whose past work has dramatically improved our everyday life in most of the world. And yet the public is growing uneasy about the same enterprise[s] from which it benefits so greatly.

Clough (2011, p. 46) also notes that, "the sheer volume of knowledge, *from not only enterprise of science, of business and of politics,* has triggered the viral growth of specialization, dividing that knowledge into smaller and smaller pieces understood by fewer and fewer people". It has further led to a major diffraction of the intellectual terrain in the production of knowledge by these enterprises and a growing disciplinary distance between them. As a result, the boundaries between these enterprises have degenerated into what could be perceived as a self-absorbed, self-serving and self-aggrandizing clutch of siloed vessels of knowledge, which fail to responsibly lead discourse on thorny development issues of our increasingly interconnected and complex world.

In fact, the Earth and atmospheric scientists assert that today the planet has entered a new geological time period dubbed "the Anthropocene" (Crutzen and Stoermer, 2000; Zalasiewicz *et al.*, 2010; Revkin, 2011). The Anthropocene is described as a time when human activities have such a profound impact on the environment that they become a primary driver of change in the Earth's natural systems. In essence, our survival as a species is now in our own hands. Yet, our sources of knowledge from enterprises of science, business and politics seem to lack a unified and holistic background needed to appreciate the choices we face in our increasingly interconnected and complex world. For the most part, they are unable, or unwilling on their own, to engage in the necessary dialogue to set in motion what McIntosh (2013) dubbed, "the necessary transition" for transformative change toward a just and sustainable world. They simply exhibit siloed, fragmented sources of knowledge propagated by current artificial disciplinary boundaries as opposed to unity of knowledge required to lead this much-needed transition. What is clear is that this much-needed transition can only be achieved by unifying different sources of knowledge—for example, science, business and politics—for human progress and development. It is at this juncture that responsible leaders of the calibre of Chief Mohlomi are needed today in order to build bridges between the current fragmented sources of knowledge. First, to assist the general public to understand the onslaught of new scientific developments; and second, to provide education in the fields of science, business and politics in order to enable them to participate more fully in the public debate relating to the cost and benefits of these sources of knowledge. The reality is that leadership for human progress and development is fraught with responsibilities that are not bound within a single source of knowledge, whether from enterprise of science, business or politics.

Against this background, by drawing on lessons largely from the history of southern Africa in the 1800s, this paper presents Mohlomi as a responsible leader whose work had pioneered unity of sources of knowledge production. This knowledge was gained from the enterprises of science, business, and politics for human progress and development in southern Africa during his time. It also provides an account of Mohlomi's approach and contribution to the study of the enterprises of science, business and politics in the 1800s that until that time had never been seen and experienced before throughout southern Africa. It further argues that Mohlomi deserves our profound recognition for showing the way to imagine a liberated and sustainable future for southern Africa by integrating different sources of knowledge from and across enterprises of science, business and politics, which transformed the society of his time. To achieve its aforementioned aims, the paper provides a brief biography of Mohlomi, in order to appreciate his noble efforts to unify knowledge between enterprises of science, of business and of politics in southern Africa in the 18th century. This is followed by a discussion of Mohlomi's work in pioneering unity of knowledge and the lessons that can be learned. There follows a discussion of some aspects of Mohlomi's work that would be problematic in contemporary times and finally, concluding remarks.

A brief biography of Mohlomi as a responsible leader of his time

Mohlomi was a Mosotho chief born around 1720 at Fothane near the present-day town of Fouriesburg in the Free State Province of the Republic of South Africa, north of modern-day Lesotho (Machobane, 1978; Ellenberger, 1912). He was born during the great migration of the Basotho (people of Lesotho today) in search of suitable settlement in southern Africa in the 1700s, which was more limited at the time than the modern-day southern Africa defined as the Southern Africa Development Community (SADC). Wars for status and power, which resulted in dissolution of emerging political groupings, characterized the migration period of Mohlomi's time in southern Africa. In fact, he lost his father, Monyane, and brother, Nkopane, to these wars. For him, these wars were simply "a needless and self-defeating way of life" (Machobane, 1978, p. 9) that he deeply abhorred.

Mohlomi lived at Ngoliloe (i.e. where one has written) near the present town of Ficksburg in the Free State Province, also north of modern-day Lesotho (Du Preez, 2012, 2004, 2003; Machobane, 1978; Bruwer, 1956; Ellenberger, 1912). This was where Mohlomi's chieftaincy headquarters were as he presided over his Basotho chiefdoms. It was also the place where he established his leadership academy where "lessons on the art of governing men" were taught for the aspiring would-be leaders (Du Preez, 2012, 2004, 2003; Machobane, 1978; Bruwer, 1956; Ellenberger, 1912). One of his famous students at his leadership academy was King Moshoeshoe, the founder of the Basotho nation in modern-day Lesotho (Du Preez, 2012, 2004, 2003; Machobane, 1978; Bruwer, 1956; Ellenberger, 1912). Mohlomi ultimately met his death in his home-village of Ngoliloe at the age of 96 years (Ellenberger and Macgregor, 1912, p. 96).

While his contemporaries made their names in the annals of history in the battlefield, Mohlomi was a celebrated doctor (traditional healer); an insatiable yet positive traveller; a rain-maker (rain-forecaster); a political consultant; a polygamy theoretician and practitioner; a philosopher; a king; and a prophet (Machobane, 1978, p. 5). Mohlomi first made his mark in his society as a doctor (*ngaka*) and rain-maker (*moroka-pula*) (Machobane, 1978, p. 9). Due to fulfilling these prominent roles, Mohlomi developed a good reputation throughout southern Africa. Mbiti (1990, p. 221) captures the importance of African traditional doctors in general thus, "[The] medicine-man applies both physical and 'spiritual' (or psychological) treatment, which assures the sufferer that all is and will be well. The medicine-man is in effect both doctor and pastor to the sick." Similarly, the importance of rain-making is recorded by Ellenberger and Macgregor (1912, p. 255). The authors stated that,

> Rain and drought were such important factors in the lives of the early Basotho, when it was not possible to make up for a bad harvest by importing grain from elsewhere… Not only did the crop fail, but cattle died of thirst. In these conditions, it is not [rocket science] that a man who was believed to be able to make rain was held in high repute (Ellenberger and Macgregor, 1912, p. 255).

Rain-making refers to use of indigenous traditional knowledge to forecast or predict rain based on the moon's shape, wind and cloud movements, lightning, animal behaviour, bird movements and so on.

As a doctor and rain-maker (i.e. rain-forecaster), Mohlomi travelled for two primary reasons: 1) on calls for healing and rain-making services (Machobane, 1978, pp. 12-13); and 2) in search of knowledge and remedies (Macgregor, 1905, p. 13). As a keen political observer, his medicine and rain-making travels enabled him also to preach peace and resolve conflicts through peaceful means in societies he visited. Here, in all villages which he visited, he would settle the differences between people when they asked him to and he entered into treaties of alliance with the chiefs, recommending them in order to cultivate peace (Arbousset and Daumas, 1846, p. 281). As a messenger of peace, he practised polygamy chiefly for social and political reasons. Socially, he married women on behalf of bachelors that did not have the necessary head of cattle to marry their own wives (Ellenberger and Macgregor, 1912, p. 97). Politically, he saw polygamy as a peaceful means of cementing friendship among polities (Machobane, 1978, p. 13). Machobane (1978, p. 13), a renowned Mosotho historian, is convinced that Mohlomi had more theoretical reasons than biological ones for practicing polygamy as the messenger of peace. This view was supported by well-known Basotho historians who saw Mohlomi as "a man of goodwill and humanity" (Macgregor, 1905, p. 13) and "a man of much benevolence" (Machobane, 1978, p. 14).

As a chief, Mohlomi's conduct of the political affairs of the people of *Monaheng* (one of the Basotho tribes in Lesotho) was viewed as "admirable and exemplary" (Machobane, 1978, p. 16), and "his government was that of a prince distinguished for clemency and wisdom" (Arbousset and Daumas, 1846, pp. 272-275). As a sage, Mohlomi was considered during his lifetime as "the wisest man that had ever lived" (Machobane, 1978, p. 17). His witty aphorisms like "medicine for a village is a good heart" and "it is better to grow corn than to brandish the spear", which spelled the themes of peace and justice, showed his sagacious frame of mind on socio-political matters. As a philosopher, Mohlomi is credited for playing a role in science, business and politics, which were outside the scope of Basotho collective wisdom at the time (Machobane, 1978, p. 18). Further, Mohlomi's prophecies made him renowned throughout southern Africa. He is credited for having prophesied the great wars of *lifagane* (i.e. the crushing or scattering of the early 1900s that changed the geo-political landscape of southern Africa) while on his deathbed (Ellenberger and Macgregor, 1912, p. 97). Such was the end of Mohlomi, "th[e] man who was the most famous of all Basot[ho]—famous for his love of peace, his charity to all, his wisdom and for the love he bore to all men" (Ellenberger and Macgregor, 1912, p. 97).

Therefore, Mohlomi as responsible leader was viewed with awe and respect during his time by many people of southern Africa. In fact, he remains a very prominent figure in southern Africa's responsible leadership history. Here, specific reference is given to his work in pioneering unity of knowledge across enterprises of science, business and politics, regarding human progress and development. He is also regarded as one of the best examples of the brilliance of pre-colonial African intellectualism in responsible leadership in southern Africa (Machaobane, 1978; du Preez, 2003). Given Mohlomi's prominent reputation and legacy, in what follows, the paper examines the socio-political problems of his time that honed his theoretical orientation and intellectualism in responsible leadership during pre-colonial southern Africa.

Mohlomi's work in pioneering unity of knowledge from different sources

The nexus between enterprises of science, business and politics as sources of knowledge, in our increasingly interconnected and complex world, cannot be overemphasized. Science, in its strict modern sense, is the systematic enterprise that builds and organizes knowledge in the form of testable explanations, observations and predictions about the universe (Wilson, 1998; Heilbron, 2003; Lindberg, 2007). This is a key contemporary definition of science against which Mohlomi's cultural "scientific" efforts of rain-making or rain-forecasting in the enterprise of science of his time should not be judged. As Lemke (2001, p. 311) correctly points out:

> In a large sense, all scientific explanations belong to a culture of science at the particular point in time, a culture that seeks particular kinds of knowledge for particular purposes. The cultures of the everyday life all seek knowledge and explanations, but often for quite different purposes; their criteria of validity also correspond different[ly].

So, it is in this regard that science should be understood in the cultural context of Mohlomi's era as, "a very human activity whose focus of interest and theoretical dispositions in a historical period were, and are, very much a part of and not apart from the dominant cultural issues of the day" (Lemke, 2001, p. 298). This is the view that contemporary science research and studies by historians, sociologists and cultural anthropologists advocate (Lemke, 2001, pp. 297-298), which the paper adopts when discussing Mohlomi's work within the enterprise of science during his time.

Business broadly refers to the commercial activity of buying and selling commodities or services with the intention of creating wealth (Sullivan and Sheffrin, 2003). Politics, in its broadest sense, is the activity through which people make, preserve and amend the general rules under which they live (Hay, 2002; Leftwich, 2004). There is no doubt that there is a beneficial relationship between these enterprises of knowledge production irrespective of their cultural frameworks. Each enterprise relies on the other for its growth and progress. They are thus termed as interdependent enterprises of knowledge production. This interdependence between these sources of knowledge was realized by Mohlomi during his time as he canvassed for unity of knowledge between and across them, and indeed, became the symbol of that advocacy throughout his lifetime.

As a renowned *Ngaka* (traditional healer) and *Moroka-pula* (rain-forecaster) of his time, Mohlomi's work within the enterprise of science of healing and rain-forecasting was natural. He travelled, seeking new cultural medicines, healing texts and cures (Guma, 1967, p. 82). According to Guma (1967), due to his travels, he became renowned for his cultural knowledge in the enterprise of the science of healing and rain-forecasting. Through his travels, he learned cultural methods and applications of healing and rain-forecasting practices from a wide variety of sources across cultures (Guma, 1967). He therefore created cultural frameworks for broad understanding of the science of cultural healing and rain-forecasting as enterprises of knowledge. This led him to become famous for his outstanding skills in the treatment of illnesses and rain-forecasting throughout southern Africa. As a *Ngaka* with a vast knowledge of natural medicine, he is said to have had a cure for leprosy and mental illness (Du Preez, 2004, p. 51). His contribution to the science of healing as an enterprise of knowledge in cultural medicine throughout southern Africa is well recorded (Ellenberger and Macgregor, 1912; Guma, 1960; Mokhehle, 1976; Machobane, 1978). He is said to have created cultural and institutional frameworks for broad understanding and social appreciation of the science of healing in southern Africa of his time. He seemed to have had a therapeutic rationale behind his cultural healing practices where among others he is said to have used herbs and psychological support to achieve optimum healing (Lesotho News Agency, 2010). His new approach to the science of healing and the methods he applied thus radicalized healing in cultural medicine as was known in the social circles of his time. He was regarded as the greatest healer of his time with immense knowledge of healing in cultural medicine. In fact, the popular tradition postulates that he was an outstanding indigenous healer whose wisdom in cultural medicine surpassed that of other healers of his time. The popular tradition further stated that he would have been comfortable with the modern science of healing as it entails the very practices, i.e. hygiene, counselling etc., that he valued, canvassed and propagated. As a *moroka-pula*, he is said to have surpassed even the Bushmen (Ellenberger and Macgregor, 1912). Thus, as a *moraka-pula*, he seemed to have studied the weather and knew how to read the weather and clouds, and thus in turn predicted when it would rain.

Naturally, Mohlomi's encounter with the enterprise of business was closely intertwined with his healing, rain-making (rain-forecasting) and teaching professions. Fees obtained from his calls for healing and rain-forecasting services (Machobane, 1978, pp. 12-13) allowed him to add substantially to his wealth repository. He managed his healing and rain-forecasting professions in a business-like manner, making him the wealthiest man of his time in his region (van Wyk, 1996, p. 22; Rosenberg and Weisfelder, 2013, p. 350). His love for the enterprise of business caused him to encourage habits of thrift and industry among his people. Here, he opposed the cultural practice of cattle raiding expeditions as a source of building wealth by seizing cattle from others. In his view, the practice was "a nonsensical, needless and self-defeating way of life" (Machobane, 1978, p. 9). It is said that he disbanded his fighting units telling the warriors to grow food and take care of women and children rather than engage in war. His aphorisms were that, "it is better to thrash the sorghum than to sharpen the spear" and "it is better to grow corn than to brandish the spear". Thus, these aphorisms spelled the themes of thrift and industry that showed his business-like frame of mind. In one of his teachings, it is said that his advice to Moshoeshoe, the famous King of the Basotho who came to him for counsel, was: "'Peace is plenty' where he added that 'At all times, I beseech you, lean upon this rod of peace' *for thrift and industry*" (Mokhehle, 1976, p. 32).

In addition, Mohlomi also accumulated wealth from tuition services he provided at his leadership academy where he trained many young and aspirant chiefs. His most famous student was Moshoeshoe, later founder and king of the Basotho nation and the man who brought stability to southern Africa during the turbulent 1820s (Couzens, 2003, p. 45; Oliver and Atmore, 2005, p. 108). Mohlomi, whose fame had spread all over southern Africa, taught him that the wise ruler sought to live in peaceful coexistence with his neighbours and encouraged habits of thrift and industry among his people.

Mohlomi was also a passionate social reformer, political consultant and tutor within the enterprise of politics in southern Africa (Machobane, 1978). His teachings and work in political thought remain instructive points of departure today. Here, he is credited for his remarkable contributions to the study of leadership, social and political behaviours in southern Africa. As a keen political observer, his rising political star in the enterprise of politics first shone within *Bamonaheng* of the dominant branch of *Bakoena*, one of the nucleus people who formed the nation of Basotho. It said that he gained political prominence in the eyes of all chieftaincies of *Bamonaheng* who badly needed the political direction that he provided. The popular tradition also tells that his conduct of the political affairs of the people of *Bamonaheng* was admirable and exemplary (Machobane, 1978, p. 16), and "his government was that of a prince distinguished for clemency and wisdom..." (Arbousset and Daumas, 1846, pp. 272-275).

As a political leadership consultant, Mohlomi had a passionate interest in the problems of government and governance issues of his time (du Preez, 2003, p. 16; Machobane, 1978, p. 13). Here, popular tradition further stated that he was typically concerned about southern Africa's governance problems of abuse of power, hostility and conflicts together with human rights abuses, especially those directed to women (Machobane, 1978). His contribution to the art of governance was the unusual political philosophy he practised and preached. The canons of his political philosophy included, but were not limited to: 1) a policy of democracy better captured by his famous saying *"morena ke morena ka sechaba"* [i.e. a chief is a chief by the grace of his people]; 2) a policy of peace as fundamental to all good and lasting governments; 3) a policy of leading people by gentleness; 4) a policy of benevolence towards the distressed; and 5) a policy of diplomatic immunity that messengers between chiefs should never be attacked and tortured, but should be given food and shelter, and be helped on their way. His political philosophy thus implied a different philosophy of leadership formulated by shared authority as leitmotif of popular governance, which was unheard of and simply absent in southern Africa at the time (Mahao, 2010, p. 322). His new political philosophy prescribed that humility, fairness and empathy had to be the stock-in-trade qualities of leadership, of social and of political behaviours for the management of public affairs.

During his lifetime, Mohlomi played a significant role in the field of politics that was outside the scope of collective wisdom in southern Africa (Machobane, 1978; Gill, 1993; du Preez, 2003). According to Gill (1993, pp. 24, 59),

> From his studies of leadership, of social and of political behaviours, [Mohlomi] developed a philosophy [of life] which he practiced and passed on to his disciples.

Here, Mohlomi's political heritage was fully applied and practised by Moshoeshoe, the founder of the Basotho nation (du Preez, 2003, p. 16). Moshoeshoe therefore famously built a nation on the political ideals propounded, canvassed and popularized by Mohlomi (Mokhehle, 1976, pp. xvi-xviii). In addition, Mohlomi prophesied a great future for Moshoeshoe that started him off on a road from which he never swerved. He therefore embraced and lived by these political philosophies and prophesies of Mohlomi as a leader during his leadership in southern Africa.

Lessons from Mohlomi's aspects of knowledge from science, business and politics

Scholars in responsible leadership advocate the importance of balanced morality: 1) to enable the development of individual and collective leadership and practice that is globally responsible; and 2) to ensure sustainable knowledge across enterprises of science, business and politics without compromising the livelihood of future generations (Doh and Stumpf, 2005; Maak and Pless, 2006; Waldman and Galvin, 2008). Such advocacy has long ago been the essence of

Mohlomi's responsible leadership teachings to the society of his time in southern Africa. He believed and taught that responsible leaders require a "values radar"; that is, the ability to scan knowledge developments of enterprises of science, business and politics to responsibly lead discourse on thorny development issues of our increasingly interconnected and complex world. As Gardner (1990, p. 77) notes:

> We must hope that our *today's* leaders will help us keep alive values that are not so easy to embed in laws—our feeling about individual *and collective responsibility*, about caring for others, about honor and integrity, about tolerance and mutual respect, and about *socially responsible development and* fulfillment within a framework of values.

There is no doubt that Mohlomi was a remarkable intellectual and responsible leader who gave thought to all kinds of human experience—the enterprises of science, business and politics. According to du Preez (2003), Mohlomi would have been considered as a "New Age guru" today due to his work in pioneering unity of knowledge from the enterprises of science, business and politics. While his contemporaries made their names in the annals of history in the battlefield, he however made his mark in his society of his time in southern Africa as a responsible leader. He is deservedly credited in historical sources for pioneering a transformative change toward a sustainable and equitable society of his time in southern Africa, which McIntosh (2013) has termed "the necessary transition". One of his significant statements, namely "Conscience is a true guide of a man, it shows him his duty always: if he does well it smiles on him and reproaches him if he does ill" (Gill, 1993), truly illustrates how morally grounded and balanced he was as a responsible leader of his time. His witty aphorisms like "medicine for a village is a good heart" (Couzens, 2003), which spell the themes of peace and justice also showed his responsible leadership frame of mind as a leader of his time.

Confronted by the moral ambivalences and exigencies of his time, Mohlomi took it upon himself to engage leaders of his time in dialogue on the critical issues of southern Africa's future (Ellenberger and Macgregor, 1912; Guma, 1960; Mokhehle, 1976; Machobane, 1978; Gill, 1993; du Preez, 2003). One of the obvious issues for such dialogue included the role of responsible leadership for human progress and development. Tapping from his deep-seated practical wisdom and knowledge he acquired on his travels throughout southern Africa, Mohlomi was able to create the required platform for the society which he served. This was a cultural and institutional framework for broad understanding and social appreciation of the enterprises of science, business and politics. Here, he skilfully and effectively used aspects of knowledge from these enterprises to address the social, economic and political problems of the society. He therefore took it upon himself to play a special role in transforming the social perception of these enterprises that was outside the scope of collective wisdom in southern Africa at the time. Paying special tribute to Mohlomi as a responsible leader of his own time, Ellenberger and MacGregor (1912, p. 90) write:

> He was no warrior: there are no conquests or extension of power to record; but the influence he acquired over his own people and other nations far and near was very great indeed, and, on the whole, it was an influence for good.

Thus Ellenberger and MacGregor (1912) regard him to be the most intelligent man among the Basotho of his time who developed a political philosophy from enterprises of science, business and politics, which he advocated, canvassed and practiced. Further, Gill (1993, pp. 24, 59) adds:

> His philosophy cannot be found in long manuscripts but it has been captured in maxims or proverbs which have since been passed down to succeeding generations.

Just to recap, such maxims or proverbs include but are not limited to the following:

> It is better to thrash the corn than to sharpen the spear. When thou shalt sit in judgment, let thy decisions be just. The law knows no one as a poor man. Conscience is the faithful monitor of man; it invariably shows him what his duty is. If he does well, it smiles upon him; if he does evil, it torments him. This inward guide takes us under its guidance when we leave the womb, and it accompanies us to the entrance of the tomb (Gill, 1993, p. 60; Couzens, 2003, pp. 50-51).

In all its various dimensions of sources of knowledge, Mohlomi's philosophical heritage was suitably portrayed by Moshoeshoe who remained steadfast to it. As Du Preez writes, "The philosopher's teachings made an impression on [Moshoeshoe] which was to last all his life" (2003, p. 16). Indeed, what Mohlomi thus instructed and prophesied, Moshoeshoe heeded and fulfilled. As Mokhehle (1976, p. xvi) interestingly argues

> For it is not stretching the point that what Jesus Christ was to Paul or Matthew, what Karl Marx was to Lenin or Mao Tse-tung, so was Mohlomi to Moshoeshoe and to Sebetoane. Jesus, Marx and Mohlomi laid down new principles for the recasting of human society. And Paul, Lenin and Moshoeshoe, each in his own field, built up new societies, state structures and religious institutions to make a human society a surety for man's humane existence in this world; to ensure man's security and survival in man's own society-complex, bristling with dynamic contradictions of a destructive nature.

Mohlomi laid down the philosophy of life—truthfulness, justice, peace, love, compassion, equality, tolerance, conciliation, respect, discipline, democracy, neighbourliness and friendship—as adduced from creative mental and physical experience of the Basotho society. Most of these were literally absent during Mohlomi's time in southern Africa and violent scramble for resources was the order of the day (Arbousset and Daumas, 1846, p. 131; Ellenberger and Macgregor, 1912, pp. 18-68). The scramble was accompanied by violent catastrophic wars and scandalous battles as the result of which many people were unnecessarily killed (Damane, 1976, pp. 3-4). It was during this time that Mohlomi taught that: 1) the practice of neighbourliness, virtue and disciple was the first and foremost prerequisite for the successful governance of men; and 2) "peace, goodwill and humanity" were the better alternative to "the washing of spears" in the neighbour's blood (Ellenberger and Macgregor, 1912, p. 13). Moshoeshoe built the Basotho nation on these philosophical principles propounded, canvassed and popularized by Mohlomi. As Mokhehle (1976, pp. xvi–xviii) eloquently puts it, "Mohlomi was the designer of the society of the Basotho people. Moshoeshoe, guided by Mohlomi's teachings, became the architect, the builder of the Basotho nation".

Indeed, it is not an exaggeration to conclude that his sophisticated teachings and his remarkable philosophy, which compares with the most famous philosophers of his time in West and East, was completely original, untouched by external influences. This conclusion is based on the fact that there is no evidence to suggest that Mohlomi met a Caucasian person before his death in 1815, although he knew of the presence of such settlers in the south and on the east coast in southern Africa at the time.

Some aspects of Mohlomi's work that would be problematic in our contemporary times

A discussion of Mohlomi's work in pioneering unity of knowledge from enterprises of science, business and politics for human progress and development would be void if a critique of some aspects his work is neglected. Disregarding his immense and profound contributions, an examination of some aspects of Mohlomi's work could today prove to be problematic by contemporary scholars on a number of fronts.

First and foremost, I suspect that his practice of polygamy for social and political reasons would prove problematic to modern scholars. Here, African feminists and Kantian moral philosophers would see difficulty with Mohlomi's practice of polygamy, which he practised and preached. For African feminists, polygamy is an unacceptable form of marriage. Annie Nasimiyu-Wasike as an African feminist, for example, argues that even traditional rationales for polygamy show it to be an arrangement for the sake of men (1992, pp. 108-18). She adds that, "polygamous relationships have crippled both men and women, and that this domestic institution is a sign of human brokenness" (Nasimiyu-Wasike, 1992, pp. 107, 116). Farley (2006, p. 87) eloquently captures Nasimiyu-Wasike's rejection of polygamy thus:

> It represents men's search for progeny and immorality; it sees women as dependent on men, yet made for the sexual and economic service to men; it identifies women's worth with child-bearing; it yields not harmony but conflict between women as co-wives; it subordinates some women to other women.

For Kantians, polygamy is not morally permitted, and in their view, it is only monogamy that can enable rightful sexual relations or shared personal lives (Denis, 2001; Varden, 2007). Or as Fennis (2008) eloquently puts it, "[it is] only monogamy [that] can realize the teleological goods of marriage". Their inference of the practice of polygamy despite its "noble" social and political reasons during Mohlomi's era would be that it simply disrespects women's autonomy (Kant, 1996) and dignity (Gaffney-Rhys, 2011, p. 1) by promoting sexual inequality. Essentially, they would argue that the practice suggests that women are mere things: 1) they are merely objects in the game of politics; and 2) they are a means to a political end, rather than an end in and of themselves (Kant, 1996). In this regard, they would even question Mohlomi's credentials as a champion of women's human rights and abuses against them (Mokhehle, 1976), which he preached during his time. However, when taking into account his approach to the practice given the era of his time, there is dissonance in what he practised and preached.

To be precise, marriage by and large was a community choice not necessarily a matter of individual choice by an individual woman during Mohlomi's era. However, in today's society, to advocate the practice of polygamy, other keen scholars would go to the extent of labelling Mohlomi an irresponsible leader from a human rights perspective In this regard, Gaffney-Rhys (2011, p. 1) contends that:

> Although polygamy is not expressly prohibited by any international instrument, it is implicitly forbidden because it discriminates against women and violates their right to dignity. Furthermore the actual practice of polygyny often contravenes other rights of women contained in those treaties e.g. the right to privacy.

Similarly, in disapproval of Mohlomi's practice of polygamy, it is said Dr Ellenberger of the Paris Evangelical Mission Society mission to the Basotho, once remarked that it was "to be regretted that a man otherwise so enlightened as Mohlomi should have shown an example of sexual irregularity, and have given rise to a polygamy which killed the consciences of those who gave themselves up to it" (Du Preez, 2004, p. 51).

Closely related to the above viewpoint, I also suspect that his capitalist (business orientated) character, which made him the wealthiest man of his time, would have received criticism from Marxist-oriented scholars. The Marxist view is that some public or social goods, such as caring and education, ought not to be for sale or to be treated as if they were a tradeable commodity for profit-making (Rigi, 2012; Marx, 1978). They would therefore have difficulty with Mohlomi's glaring capitalist ethic tendencies that made him run the professions of healing, rain-making and teaching in a business-like manner, making him rich. Marxists would argue that healthcare and education are fundamental social goods and that deriving profit from them entrenches inequality in society (Larkin, 2011, p. 20; Covington, 2008, p. 233). In fact, Marxists would argue that the capitalist ethic he displayed as a businessman of his time potentially set up a rather uncomfortable dissonance in his philosophy of life that he advocated and preached. They would further argue that the capture of these public goods by the wealthy would seem to them to be a step away from the practice of basic principles of equity, which are supposedly attributed to his philosophy of life. They might even argue that deriving profit from education and healthcare is a human rights abuse in itself that Mohlomi was guilty of committing. To them, this would seem to be an apparent paradox between Mohlomi's political philosophy and his business philosophy, which so strongly resonates with our present world. Although one of Mohlomi's professions (i.e. rain-making) has not persisted to the present day, in terms of the two (i.e. healing and teaching) that have persisted, there is extensive and enduring ideologically motivated Marxist debate as to whether these ought to be a source of profit (Rigi, 2012; Larkin, 2011; Covington, 2008).

Similarly, native scholars and activists like Deloria (1997) would have a problem with Mohlomi's capitalist ethic of charging payment for the provision of teaching services as a spiritual leader of his time (Kehoe, 1990; Rose 1992). As Smith (1994, p. 168) states:

> True spiritual leaders do not make a profit from their teachings, whether it's through selling books, workshops, sweat lodges, or otherwise. Spiritual leaders teach the people because it is their responsibility to pass what they have learned from their elders to the younger generations. They do not charge for their services.

In the eyes of the "native" scholars and activists, the profession of teaching is not for profit-making. Rather, it is primarily a spiritual service or good aimed at helping others to respond to challenging circumstances. In the words of Partridge, "[It] fulfils a vital role in the continuity of not only tribal culture, but of the mindset concerning people's relationship to the [spiritual and] natural world" (2010: 41). In this regard, Deloria (1997) calls traditional teachers who charge fees for teaching tribal knowledge "hawkers of spirituality". He regards this appropriation as a consequence of the capitalist ethic, which denies ordinary people from getting knowledge from "philosopher–teachers of tribal knowledge" (Deloria, 1997) of the calibre of Mohlomi.

Lastly, connected to the polygamist and capitalist dimensions of his character, I further suspect that Mohlomi's credentials of leading transformative change toward a sustainable and equitable society of his time, in socio-cultural and economic terms, would be called to question by Marxist feminist scholars (Barret, 1980; Vogel, 1983, 1995; Gimenez, 2005). They would argue that women's oppression as "the capitalist system of social organisation" did not change during Mohlomi's time. In fact, he actually reinforced women's oppression by "commoditizing them as tradeable goods" for social and political expediency (Ellenberger and Macgregor, 1912, p. 97; Machobane, 1978, p. 13). In this regard, the Marxist feminists would argue that the continued oppression of women through his conduct and actions was not geared towards transformative change. To them, it would seem to be a step away from transformative change toward a sustainable and equitable society, which he supposedly championed in his philosophy of life.

Indeed, Mohlomi seems to have been truly "a man for all seasons", whose critics would argue that he ignored his own moral compass contained in his philosophy of life for social, business and political expediency gains. That said, however, there is no denying that Mohlomi's teachings are still urgent and present today.

Conclusion

Close study of Mohlomi as a pioneer in bridging knowledge from enterprises of science, business and politics in southern Africa in the 18th century adds to our current understanding of the importance of responsible leadership in human progress and development. Here, his insightful perspectives and an uncompromising position regarding major issues confronting the society of his time was examined, where he used his insights into the enterprises of science, business and politics to bring about the necessary transition for human progress and development in southern Africa. This paper showed that due to his wisdom, courage, commitment and integrity as a leader, Mohlomi deserves our profound recognition. His pioneering work thus showed that leadership is fraught with responsibilities that are not bounded in a single source of knowledge, whether science, business or politics.

The paper is not necessarily purporting that Mohlomi is the highest authority in pioneering unity of knowledge from the enterprises of science, business and politics perspective in order to improve human progress and development in southern Africa. It simply tries to open up new vistas, to transcend prevailing assumptions and paradigms by entering, and taking into account different ways of thinking from our current times. So, the readers of this paper should take it as an experiment testing whether some issues in responsible leadership can be illuminated by hypothetically removing the notion that renowned thinkers from the past like Mohlomi are fundamentally circumscribed by the exigencies of their time, and instead attending to their every word as something that possibly speaks to us in our contemporary times.

References

Arbousset, T., & Daumas, F. (1846). *Narrative of an Exploratory Tour of the North-East of the Colony of the Cape of Good Hope*. Cape Town: AS Robertson.

Barrett, M. (1980). *Women Oppression Today: The Marxist Feminist Encounter*. London: Verso Books.

Clough, G. W. (2011). *Increasing Scientific Literacy: A Shared Responsibility*. Retrieved from http://www.scifun.org/news/Increasing-Scientific-Literacy-a-Shared-Responsibility.pdf

Convington, P. (2008). *Success in Sociology: A's Student Book AQA*. Dublin: Folens Publishers.

Couzens, T. (2003). *Murder at Morija*. Johannesburg: Random House.

Crutzen, P.J., & Stoermer, E. F. (2000). The Anthropocene. *Global Change Newsletter*, 41, 17–18.

Deloria, V. Jr. (1997). *Red Earth and White Lies*. Golden: Fulcrum Publishing.

Denis, L. (2001). From friendship to marriage: Revising Kant. *Philosophy and Phenomenological Research*, 63, 1-28.

Doh, J.P., & Stumpf, S.A. (2005). *Handbook on Responsible Leadership and Governance in Global Business*. Cheltenham: Edward Elgar.

Du Preez, M. (2003). *Pale Native Memories of a Renegade Reporter*. Cape Town: Zebra Press.

Du Preez, M. (2004). *Of Warriors, Lovers and Prophets: Unusual Stories from South Africa's Past*. Cape Town: Zebra Press.

Ellenberger, D.F., & MacGregor, J.C. (1912). *History of the Basuto: Ancient and Modern*. London: Caxton.

Farley, M.A. (2006). *Just Love: A Framework of Christian Sexual Ethics*. New York: Continuum.

Fennis, S. (2008). "Marriage: A basic and exigent good." *Monist*, 91, 388-406.

Gaffney-Rhys, R. (2011). "Polygamy: Human right or human rights". *Women in Society*, 2, 1-13.

Gardner, J.W. (1990). *On Leadership*. New York: The Free Press.

Gill, S. J. (1993). *A Short History of Lesotho*. Morija: Morija Museum and Archives.

Gimenez, M.E. (2005). "Capitalism and the oppression of women: Marx revisited". *Science and Society*, 69 (1), 11 – 32.

Guma, S.M. (1960). *Morena Mohlomi Mor'a Monyane*. Pietermaritzburg: Shuter and Shooter.

Guma, S.M. (1967). *The Form, Content, and Technique of Traditional Literature in Southern Sotho*. Pretoria: Van Schaik.

Hay, C. (Ed.). (2010). *New Directions in Political Science: Responding to the Challenge of an Independent World*. Basingstoke: Palgrave.

Heilbron, J. L. (Ed.) (2003). *The Oxford Companion to the History of Modern Science*. New York: Oxford University Press.

Kant, I. (1996). The Metaphysics of Morals. In M.J. Gregor (Ed.) *Immanuel Kant: Practical Philosophy*. (pp. 353-603). New York: Cambridge University Press.

Kehoe, A. B. (1990). Primal Gaia: Primitivists and Plastic Medicine Men. In: J. Clifton, (Ed.) *The Invented Indian: Cultural Fictions and Government Policies* (pp. 193-209). New Brunswick, NJ: Transaction Publishers.

Larkin, M. (2011). *Social Aspects of Health, Illness and Healthcare*. Berkshire: Open University Press.

Leftwich, A. (Ed.) (2004). *What is Politics? The Activity and Its Study*. Cambridge: Polity Press Ltd.

Lemke, J.L. (2001). Articulating communities: Socio-cultural perspective on science education. *Journal of Research in Science Teaching*, 38 (3), 296-316.

Lesotho News Agency. (2010, March 25). *Mohlomi memorial lecture reveals Basotho's healing art*. Retrieved from www.gov.ls/articles/2010/mohlomi_memorial_lecture.php.

Lindberg, D.L. (2007). *The Beginnings of Western Science: the European Scientific Tradition in Philosophical, Religious, and Institutional Context*. (2nd Ed.). Chicago: University of Chicago Press.

Maak, T. & Pless, N.M. (Eds.) (2006). *Responsible Leadership*. London: Routledge.

Macgregor, J.C. (1905). *Basuto Traditions*. Cape Town: Willem Hiddingh.

McIntosh, M. (Ed.). (2013). *The Necessary Transition: The Journey Towards the Sustainable Enterprise Economy*. Sheffield: Greenleaf Publishing Limited.

Machobane, L.B.J. (1978). Mohlomi: Doctor, Traveller and Sage. *Mohlomi, Journal of Southern African Historical Studies*, 2, 5-27.

Mahao, N.L. (2010). "O se re ho morwa 'morwa towe!' African jurisprudence exhumed". *XLIII CILSA*, 43 (3), 317-336.

Marsh, D., & Stoker, G. (Eds.) (2010). *Theory and Methods in Political Science*. (3rd edition). New York: Palgrave Macmillan.

Marx, K. (1978). 'Preface to A Contribution to the Critique of Political Economy'. In Tucker, R.C. (Ed.) *Marx and Engels Reader*, (pp. 3-6). New York: Norton and Company.

Mokhehle, N. (1976). *Moshoeshoe 1 Profile Se-Moshoeshoe*. Maseru: Mmoho Publications.

Oliver, R., & Atmore, A. (2005). *Africa since 1800* (5th Ed.). Cambridge: Cambridge University Press.

Partridge, C. (2010). "Residential schools: The intergenerational impacts of aboriginal peoples". *Native Social Work Journal*, 7, 33-62.

Revkin, A.C. (2011). Confronting the 'Anthropocene'. *New York Times*. Retrieved from http://dotearth.blogs.nytimes.com/2011/05/11/confronting-the-anthropocene/

Rickless, S. (2005). Polygamy and Same-Sex Marriage: A Response to Calhoun. *San Diego Law Review*, 42, 1047-1048.

Rigi, R. (2012). 'Peer to Peer production as the alternative to capitalism: a new communist horizon'. *Journal of Peer Production*, Retrieved from http://www.indymedia.org.uk/en/2012/08/498544.html.

Rose, W. (1992). "The Great Pretenders: Further Reflections on White Shamanism." In: Jaimes, M. A., (ed.). *The State of Native America: Genocide, Colonisation and Resistance*. (pp. 403-421), Boston: South End.

Rosenberg, S. and Weisfelder, R. F. (2013). *Historical Dictionary of Lesotho*. Maryland: Scarecrow Press.

Savigny, H., & Marsden, L. (2011). *Doing Political Science and International Relations: Theories in Action.* London: Palgrave Macmillan.

Smith, A. (1994). "For All Those Who Were Indian in a Former life." In: Adams, C. (Ed.). *Ecofeminism and the Sacred* (pp. 168-171), New York: Continuum.

Strauss, G. (2012). "Is polygamy Inherently Unequal?" *Ethics,* 122, 516-544.

Sullivan, A., & Sheffrin, S. M. (2003). *Economics: Principles in Action.* New Jersey: Upper Saddle River.

Van Wyk, G. (1996). *Basotho.* New York: The Rosen Publishing Group, Inc.

Varden, H. (2007). "A Kantian Conception of Rightful Sexual Relations: Sex (Gay), Marriage and Prostitution". *Social Philosophy Today,* 22, 199 – 218.

Vogel, L. (1983). *Marxism and the Oppression of Women: Toward a Unitary Theory.* New Brunswick: Rutgers University Press.

Vogel, L. (1995). *Woman Questions: Essays for a Materialist Feminism.* New York: Routledge.

Waldman, D. A., & Galvin, B. M. (2008). Alternative Perspectives of Responsible Leadership. *Organizational Dynamics,* 37 (4), 327-341.

Wilson, E. O. (1998). *Consilience: The Unity of Knowledge.* New York: Vintage Books.

Zalasiewicz, J., Williams, M., Steffen, W., & Crutzen, P. (2010). The New World of the Anthropocene. *Environment Science and Technology,* 44 (7), 2228–2231.

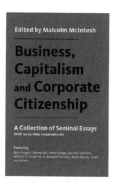
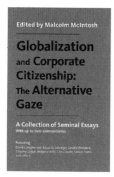

About the Journal of Corporate Citizenship

THE JOURNAL OF CORPORATE CITIZENSHIP (*JCC*) is a multidisciplinary peer-reviewed journal that focuses on integrating theory about corporate citizenship with management practice. It provides a forum in which the tensions and practical realities of making corporate citizenship real can be addressed in a reader-friendly, yet conceptually and empirically rigorous format.

JCC aims to publish *the best ideas integrating the theory and practice of corporate citizenship in a format that is readable, accessible, engaging, interesting and useful* for readers in its already wide audience in business, consultancy, government, NGOs and academia. It encourages practical, theoretically sound, and (when relevant) empirically rigorous manuscripts that address real-world implications of corporate citizenship in global and local contexts. Topics related to corporate citizenship can include (but are not limited to): corporate responsibility, stakeholder relationships, public policy, sustainability and environment, human and labour rights/ issues, governance, accountability and transparency, globalisation, small and medium-sized enterprises (SMEs) as well as multinational firms, ethics, measurement, and specific issues related to corporate citizenship, such as diversity, poverty, education, information, trust, supply chain management, and problematic or constructive corporate/human behaviours and practices.

In addition to articles linking the theory and practice of corporate citizenship, *JCC* also encourages innovative or creative submissions (for peer review). Innovative submissions can highlight issues of corporate citizenship from a critical perspective, enhance practical or conceptual understanding of corporate citizenship, or provide new insights or alternative perspectives on the realities of corporate citizenship in today's world. Innovative submissions might include: critical perspectives and controversies, photography, essays, poetry, drama, reflections, and other innovations that help bring corporate citizenship to life for management practitioners and academics alike.

JCC welcomes contributions from researchers and practitioners involved in any of the areas mentioned above. Manuscripts should be written so that they are comprehensible to an intelligent reader, avoiding jargon, formulas and extensive methodological treatises wherever possible. They should use examples and illustrations to highlight the ideas, concepts and practical implications of the ideas being presented. Theory is important and necessary; but theory—with the empirical research and conceptual work that supports theory—needs to be balanced by integration into practices to stand the tests of time and usefulness. *JCC* aims to be the premier journal to publish articles on corporate citizenship that accomplish this integration of theory and practice. We want the journal to be read as much by executives leading corporate citizenship as it is by academics seeking sound research and scholarship.

JCC appears quarterly and includes peer-reviewed papers by leading writers, with occasional reviews, case studies and think-pieces. A key feature is the 'Turning Points' section. Turning Points are commentaries, controversies, new ideas, essays and insights that aim to be provocative and engaging, raise the important issues of the day and provide observations on what is too new yet to be the subject of empirical and theoretical studies. *JCC* continues to produce occasional issues dedicated to a single theme. These have included 'Story Telling: Beyond the Academic Article—Using Fiction, Art and Literary Techniques to Communicate', 'Sustainable Luxury', 'Business–NGO Partnerships', 'Creating Global Citizens and Responsible Leadership', 'Responsible Investment in Emerging Markets', 'The Positive Psychology of Sustainable Enterprise', 'Textiles, Fashion and Sustainability', 'Designing Management Education', 'Managing by Design' and 'Innovative Stakeholder.

EDITORS

General Editor:

Professor Malcolm McIntosh; email: jcc@greenleaf-publishing.com

Regional Editor:

North American Editor: Sandra Waddock, Professor of Management, Boston College, Carroll School of Management, Senior Research Fellow, Center for Corporate Citizenship, Chestnut Hill, MA 02467 USA; tel: +1 617 552 0477; fax: +1 617 552 0433; email: waddock@bc.edu

Notes for Contributors

SUBMISSIONS

All content should be submitted via online submission. For more information see the journal homepage at www.greenleaf-publishing.com/jcc.

The form gives prompts for the required information and asks authors to submit the full text of the paper, including the title, author name and author affiliation, as a Word attachment. **Abstract and keywords will be completed via the online submission and are not necessary on the attachment.**

As part of the online submission authors will be asked to tick a box to state they have read and adhere to the Greenleaf–GSE Copyright Guidelines and have permission to publish the paper, including all figures, images, etc. which have been taken from other sources. It is the author's responsibility to ensure this is correct.

In order to be able to distribute papers published in Greenleaf journals, we need signed transfer of copyright from the authors. We are committed to a liberal and fair approach to copyright and accessibility, and do not restrict authors' rights to reuse their own work for personal use or in an institutional repository.

A brief autobiographical note should be supplied at the end of the paper including:

- Full name
- Affiliation
- Email address
- Full international contact details

Please supply (via online submission) an **abstract outlining the title, purpose, methodology and main findings**. It's worth considering that, as your paper will be located and read online, the quality of your abstract will determine whether readers go on to access your full paper. We recommend you place particular focus on the impact of your research on further research, practice or society. What does your paper contribute?

In addition, please provide up to **six descriptive keywords**.

Please address all new manuscripts via the online submission system to the incoming Editor for 2016-2018, David Murphy.

FORMATTING YOUR PAPER

Headings should be short and in bold text, with a clear and consistent hierarchy.

Please identify **Notes or Endnotes** with consecutive numbers, enclosed in square brackets and listed at the end of the article.

Figures and other images should be submitted as .jpeg (.jpg) or .tif files and be of a high quality. Please number consecutively with Arabic numerals and mark clearly within the body of the text where they should be placed.

If images are not the original work of the author, it is the author's responsibility to obtain written consent from the copyright holder to them being used. Authors will be asked to confirm this is the case by ticking the box on the online submission to say they have read and understood the Greenleaf–GSE copyright policy. Images which are neither the authors' own work, nor are accompanied by such permission will not be published.

Tables should be included as part of the manuscript, with relevant captions.

Supplementary data can be appended to the article, using the form and should follow the same formatting rules as the main text.

References to other publications should be complete and in Harvard style, e.g. (Jones, 2011) for one author, (Jones and Smith, 2011) for two authors and (Jones *et al.*, 2011) for more than two authors. A full reference list should appear at the end of the paper.

- For **books**: Surname, Initials (year), *Title of Book*, Publisher, Place of publication.
  e.g. Author, J. (2011), *This is my book*, Publisher, New York, NY.
- For **book chapters**: Surname, Initials (year), "Chapter title", Editor's Surname, Initials, *Title of Book*, Publisher, Place of publication, pages (if known).
- For **journals**: Surname, Initials (year), "Title of article", *Title of Journal*, volume, number, pages.
- For **conference proceedings**: Surname, Initials (year), "Title of paper", in Surname, Initials (Ed.), Title of published proceeding which may include place and date(s) held, Publisher, Place of publication, Page numbers.
- For **newspaper articles**: Surname, Initials (year) (if an author is named), "Article title", *Newspaper*, date, pages.
- For **images**:
  Where image is from a printed source—as for books but with the page number on which the image appears.
  Where image is from an online source—Surname, Initials (year), Title, Available at, Date accessed.
  Other images—Surname, Initials (year), Title, Name of owner (person or institution) and location for viewing.

▶ **To discuss ideas for contributions**, please contact the General Editor: Professor Malcolm McIntosh; email: jcc@greenleaf-publishing.com.